REFLECTIONS:
An ANXIETY, FEARS, PHOBIAS, and PTSD RECOVERY WORKBOOK

BY:

JOSHUA B. SETH

FreD.
As Promised, here is a
copy of Book 4 (CBT style).
Hope you enjoy!

JBS Publishing 2014©

Softcover ISBN-13:978-1500161682

JBS Publishing
Saint Louis, Missouri

Partnered with Create Space

Printed in the United States of America

DEDICATIONS

I would like to thank God because I would not be where I am today without Him.

> *"I can do all things through Christ who strengthens me."*
> *-- Philippians 4:13*

I would also like to thank my family and best friend Michael A. who have been supportive over the years with my recovery process. While many of them simply do not understand exactly what it must be like to walk in my shoes, they have remained supportive just the same.

I would also like to thank Dr. Saad Khan who has been with me every step of the way through my recovery; and a special thanks to Kelly Locker and Pastor John Moore (St. Louis Family Church).

ABOUT THE AUTHOR

Joshua B. Seth is a Victimologist, Activist, and former Criminologist with his BS/MS in Criminal Justice and he has graduate minors in Counseling and Gender Studies. Seth has dedicated his life to working with victims and survivors of domestic violence and intimate partner violence (IPV), sexual violence and child abuse, Post-Traumatic Stress Disorder (PTSD), bullying, and eating disorders. He is also an activist for Human Rights that includes but is not limited to Gender Rights, LGBT Rights, Civil Rights, Consumer Rights, Animal Rights, and those with mental and physical handicaps. In addition to writing self-help books, Seth is a survivor of fears, phobia, anxiety, PTSD, sexual violence, and anorexia and bulimia.

Published

(1) Reflections: An Eating Disorders Recovery Workbook (2014)
- A recovery workbook for anorexia and bulimia designed to help people in all stages of recovery.

(2) Offenders and Abuse, 2nd Ed. (2013)
- A self-help book for victims and survivors of domestic violence, intimate partner violence (IPV), sexual violence, child abuse, kidnappings, PTSD; and eating disorders as it relates to victimization.

(3) Offenders and Abuse: An Awareness Guide to Shielding the Community (2009)
- Profiling Sex Offenders and Community Awareness

TABLE OF CONTENTS

PREFACE

This book was written in an effort to help those who are struggling with anxiety, fears, phobias, and Post-Traumatic Stress Disorder. Have you ever felt so alone that you believed that nobody else could ever understand what it is that you are going through? For this reason, I have found aspects of recovery to be more helpful to others by disclosing my own personal battles with the very subjects that I talk about in my books so that others may realize that they are not alone. I am not just an educator of community awareness but I too have walked in these shoes. In this book, I openly talk about my experiences with anxiety, fears, phobias, and Post-Traumatic Stress Disorder (PTSD).

The questions and exercises in this book are designed to help those who have difficulties journaling and who struggle with anxiety, fears, phobias, and PTSD. This book is also designed to help individuals to self-identify with, who they are as a person with these disorders in a society with labels and stigmas. It is important to not let other people's negative opinions or society's labels be used to identify who you are as a person. Those types of opinions are their reality not yours. You cannot always make others accept, validate, or understand what you are going through. In the end, you only need to do what is best for you and your recovery so that you begin living in the present rather than the past.

I have created this book to help people from all stages of recovery; whether it is your first day or your one hundredth, because recovery is possible at any age in one's life.

DISCLAIMER I

I am not a professional therapist or doctor nor can I prescribe medications. That said, I have been to several therapists and have tried several medications over the years to help with my own anxiety, fears, phobias, and Post-Traumatic Stress Disorder (PTSD). In this book, I will discuss what has and has not worked for me over the years. Please remember that everyone has different body chemistries and medications will affect each of us differently. I have attended several in person support groups over the years and I have created and participated in many online support groups through Facebook. I have walked in these shoes and therefore I do know the importance of the need to talk with others who have been through similar situations rather than just talking with a professional who is merely educated on the subject.

Medication alone is not enough for one's recovery and often people need a combination of medication, therapy, spiritual guidance, meditation, etc. to aid in their healing process. As for me, I know that I will probably be taking medication for the rest of my life but this does not suggest that everyone is required to take anxiety and antidepressant medications to overcome their disorders. In addition, to taking medication, I also meditate, attend therapy, go to church on a weekly basis, and rely on positive coping skills to reduce the need for high doses of these medications.

I also know that for many people in recovery, talking about their mental problems with family, friends, or even strangers is never easy because these disorders often involves very personal issues such as a sexual assault, child abuse and other traumatic life events. For others, they may feel too embarrassed or feel judged by others if they were to disclose the intimate details of their life that has led to anxiety, fears, phobias, and PTSD.

As for my recovery process, I have felt that the next step in my recovery process was to share my fears, phobias, anxieties, and PTSD related life events so that others will see that they are not alone with their recovery. I will admit that even though I write under a pen-name, many of my former high school classmates, friends, and family members are aware of my pen-name, so I did experience a small degree of anxiety when they learned that I was a victim of sexual violence and suffered for nearly 30 years of anorexia let alone bulimia; but at the same time, once the anxiety settled down, I felt so empowered from talking openly about my life events just knowing that others could be helped. I used to live in the past thanks to my PTSD but now I am grounded and living in the present and hopeful of my future. Like many, I battled depression for many years and even hit rock-bottom too many times to count but these days, I feel so alive and so can you.

This book is not intended to diagnose or act as a substitute for treatment whether you or someone you know has been diagnosed or believes that they suffer from anxiety, fears, phobias, or Post-Traumatic Stress Disorder. This book is however, a means of help and support for those who are dealing with these disorders so that they will learn how to avoid internalizing their thoughts and emotions. The publication of this book does not institute the practice of medicine or therapeutic licensure nor substitute in place of a medical doctor or physician for treatment. I strongly recommend consulting with a licensed medical doctor that includes but is not limited to internists, pediatricians, psychiatrist, or licensed psychologists, therapists, or counselors regarding a diagnosis, or minister of prescriptions, over the counter (OTC) medications or other treatments discussed in this book.

TRIGGER WARNING

Please note that I will be talking potential triggers for some people based on their own fears, phobias, anxieties, and PTSD. The intent here is not to cause anyone to feel depressed or for them to engage in any negative coping skills; however, it is important to know that with any type of therapeutic approach, people tend to experience many types of emotions and may even feel worse in the beginning of a treatment program. This book might trigger some strong emotions; however, I am a strong believer that it is better to let the emotions out rather than to keep them bottled up inside. I do not recommend working through this entire book in one sitting. You may need to skip around to different sections of the book. There is no specific order that this book and it is designed to help people in all stages of recovery.

BASIC DEFINITIONS

FEARS

Commonly refers to any unlikeable emotion or thoughts that dwell on the belief that there is the possibility of an immediate or future threat or pain to them or others. Fears can be associated with a terrifying or terrorizing event, person, place, sound, scent, or thing. A fear of a person is often associated with emotional, physical, sexual abuse or assault. A fear of an event could be associated with a terrorist attack. For example, on 9/11/01, after both World Trade Center towers and several airplanes came crashing down as the result of a terrorist attack, there was a potential threat that similar attacks could have occurred in all major cities across the nation. This type of threat would no doubt cause many people to be scared to leave their homes or fly in airplanes for many years to come. A fear of a place could be associated with; say for example that a person survived a deadly car accident that left other passengers dead. For the person who survived such a horrific accident, it goes without saying that the location of the accident could cause dire distress to the lone survivor every time they drive by the location of the car accident. A fear of a thing is often associated with phobias such as the fear of flying, heights, darkness, dogs, etc. Fears related to sounds and scents are often delayed triggers associated with PTSD.

Fears are often the result of conditioning and learned behaviors which can be rational or irrational. Fears are often perceived as a danger to man, animal; health, status quo, personal security and/or any property that holds personal or actual value. Fear can provoke a personal perception of a ***fight or flight*** response.

PHOBIAS

Commonly refers to any irrational fear or obsession of someone or something that is tangible, defined, or indescribable. Phobias can be any overwhelming or irrational fear that is believed to be threatening but in reality has no real danger. Although, most phobias are often controllable, the effects on the person experiencing the fearful response can lead to severe anxiety and panic attacks, or the need to avoid the triggering situation all together. Many phobias can be managed through learned behaviors and positive coping skills such as mediation, yoga, journaling, or even avoiding the impending fearful situation. Still, some may need the help and guidance of a licensed therapist and/or psychiatrist and the use of prescribed antidepressants and anxiety medication. Unfortunately, there is no right method to combating phobias because everyone heals in their own way and at their own speed. Phobias that cause panic attacks can involve paralysis of the whole or specific parts of the body. Some of these effects may include numbing and tingling hands, feet, and lips; flashbacks, chills, and other psychological and physical issues such as an intense fear that the panic attack will lead to a heart attack, stroke, or death. No two people will experience the same physical or psychological effects.

COMMON PHOBIAS

PHOBIA	FEAR
Acrophobia	Heights
Aquaphobia	Water
Arachnophobia	Spiders
Claustrophobia	Closed or Confined Spaces
Mysophobia	Germs
Nyctophobia	Darkness
Pteromerhanophobia	Flying
Sociaphobia	Crowds

FIGHT OR FLIGHT SYNDROME

Commonly refers to a physical response as the result of a psychological perception of the sympathetic nervous system. This can be a natural response by the body to fight or flee based on physical conditions such as an immediate release of sweat glands dripping down the face, hands and feet; increased heart rate and blood pressure, adrenalin, dilated pupils, and an overwhelming need to either stand and fight or run as if they are being chased by a wild animal. A Fight or Flight response can be the result of facing one's fears or even choosing whether to stand up to a bully. This response often triggers an increased heart rate, muscle tension, hypersensitivity to the 5-senses, hyperventilation, perspiration, a fear cage mindset, hot flashes, and basically feeling like you have just been caught like a dear in the headlights of an oncoming vehicle as you decide whether stand there with feelings of superhuman strength or quickly move out of the way!

ANXIETY

Commonly refers to a body natural reaction to fears, phobias, stress, and other mental disorders such as obsessive compulsive disorder (OCD), panic attacks, Post-Traumatic Stress Disorder (PTSD). Anxiety can manifest whenever a person feels upset, angry, disorientated, worried, fearful, nervous, restless, agitated, apprehensive, powerless, or stressed. Anxiety can also lead to paralysis of the mind and body. Panic attacks can give the appearance and familiarity of a heart attack, stroke, or feeling of impending death. Uncontrollable anxiety can lead to disruptions in one's daily life and working conditions. Symptoms of anxiety may include tremors and shaking of specific body parts or the whole body, shortness of breath, heart palpitations, sweating, nausea, numbness and tingling of hands and fingers and feet and toes, hot flashes, fear of impending doom, psychosis, and feeling out of control, etc.

PANIC ATTACKS

Commonly refers to an intense fear that there is impending danger which can lead to hyperventilation, sweating, nervousness, paralysis, fatigue, difficulty concentrating and fear that they are having a heart attack or stroke. Some people have one or two panic attacks in their lifetime while others tend to experience them quite frequently. Phobias can manifest from a wide range of anxiety disorders, phobias and fears. Symptoms of anxiety may include tremors and shaking of specific body parts or the whole body, shortness of breath, chest pains and heart palpitations, sweating, nausea, numbness and tingling of hands and fingers and feet and toes, hot flashes, fear of impending doom, psychosis, and feeling out of control.

ANXIETY DISORDERS

Generalized Anxiety Disorder (GAD)	GAD tends to be associated with extreme and irrational worrying, stress and tension, fears and phobias, and unknown conditions; unable to control the worrying, difficulty concentrating, tense muscles, difficulty sleeping or falling asleep, and all of this causing emotional distress with relationships and working conditions; on the edge (irritability).
Obsessive Compulsive Disorder (OCD)	OCD tends to be associated with a constant need to act a certain and repetitive way; involves rituals and routines, and can cause fear and stress if they attempt to sway away from specific methods for doing things in their life (i.e.: a person who always sets their alarm clock to a specific set of numbers such as 6:46, 6:52, 7:01 will have difficulty adjusting their behaviors to set the clock to a more common time set of 6:45, 6:50, or 7:00). A person with OCD may feel the need to wash their hands 3 times every time they wash their hands. While a fear of germs tends to be a common phobia for people with OCD, they could in fact feel the need to wash their hands 3 times regardless of any fear of germs; uncontrollable obsessions, reoccurring thoughts, excessive and unreasonable actions and thoughts; unwanted racing ideas, images (similar to mania).

Panic Disorder	(see above)
Post-Traumatic Stress Disorder (PTSD)	PTSD tends to manifest as the result of a traumatic event, natural disaster, or loss of a friend, loved one, or classmate. PTSD tends to involve everlasting and terrifying flashbacks coupled with a severe Panic Attack. PTSD is the body's way of trying to understand the mind's debilitating reactions; subconsciously avoids triggers; difficulty concentrating (short term); memory problems (long term); feeling on guard and hypersensitive.

POST-TRAUMATIC STRESS DISORDER (PTSD)

Commonly refer to a severe type of anxiety disorder that can cause a great deal of emotional and physical pain as the result of severe psychological or physical trauma. Imagine an anxiety attack about 50 times worse than any normal anxiety attack. When I have a PTSD related panic attack, my body feels motionless and as if I am trapped in a fear-cage. I have chills yet my blood feels like it is boiling throughout my entire body. My anxiety feels like I am having a heart attack or stroke with my blood pressure upwards of 155/110. People around me during one of these attacks have said that I look like I am in some type of trance as I am experiencing flashbacks of my traumatic life events. The flashbacks seem to be in some type of constant loop in my mind like a broken record player repeating the same tune over and over again. Once my PTSD panic attack has passed, the actual attack itself typically lasts for about 30 seconds to a couple of minutes but I loose time and what feels as if hours not minutes have passed.

What causes PTSD?

Honestly, PTSD can manifest in anyone who has ever experiences a traumatic life event that caused them to experience severe bouts of anxiety, panic attacks with flashbacks and reoccurring nightmares and night terrors ever since the event originally occurred. For some, they may experience night terrors as opposed to the typical run of the mill nightmare. The difference between a nightmare and a night terror is with a night terror, the person tends to wake up in a terrified state of mind in which they are too scared to 'ever' go back to sleep again. The following are examples of traumatic life events that could manifest from anxiety and panic attacks to severe panic attacks and PTSD.

- ✓ Victims of Robbery with or without the use or threat of a weapon

- ✓ Victims of Carjacking

- ✓ Victims of Child Abuse

- ✓ Victims of Sexual Abuse

- ✓ Victims of Rape/Sexual Assault

- ✓ Victims of Kidnappings

- ✓ Victims of Domestic Violence / Intimate Partner Violence (IPV)

- ✓ Victims of Car Accidents regardless of the severity of the accident

- ✓ War Survivors

- ✓ Survivors of Attempted Murder

- ✓ Survivors of Attempted Assault

- ✓ The Loss of a friend or family member associated with suicide

- ✓ The Loss of a Child

- ✓ Survivors Guilt (common with soldiers and car accident survivors)

- ✓ Terrorist Attacks or Threats of Violence (i.e.: the aftermath following 9/11/01)

- ✓ Survivors/Friends/Family members of School Shootings (i.e.: Columbine Massacre 4/19/1999)

- ✓ . . .

SIGNS & SYMPTOMS OF
ANXIETY & POST-TRAUMATIC STRESS DISORDER (PTSD)

CHANGES IN EATING HABITS	▪ Emotional Eating ▪ Loss of Appetite
CHANGES IN MOOD	▪ Guilt ▪ Anger ▪ Anxiety ▪ Aggression ▪ Depression ▪ Hopelessness ▪ Hypersensitivity ▪ On the Edge Feelings ▪ Suicidal Idealizations ▪ Feeling Emotionally Numb ▪ Increased Fear or Nervousness ▪ Difficulty experiencing positive emotions ▪ Negative Thoughts/Emotions about self/others ▪ Decline in Sexual Desires, drive or performance
SLEEP BEHAVIORS	▪ Night Terrors ▪ Fear of Dying ▪ Difficulty Sleeping ▪ Scared to go to sleep ▪ Fear of never waking up ▪ Reoccurring Nightmares
FLASHBACKS (NIGHTMARES AND DAYDREAMS)	▪ Reliving traumatic events (like a scene from a movie constantly replaying) through nightmares and daydreams

SEVERE EMOTIONAL DISTRESS *(Due to:)*	▪ Names ▪ Scents ▪ Words ▪ Sounds ▪ Locations ▪ Known Trigger Objects ▪ Unknown Trigger Objects ▪ Physical Touch of Others ▪ Physical Touch by Others
ISOLATION & AVOIDANCE	▪ Avoiding known triggers ▪ Withdrawn from friends ▪ Withdrawn from favorite hobbies and activities
PERSONAL SPACE & BOUNDARY ISSUES	▪ Always on guard (hypersensitivity) ▪ A need for extended personal space with friends, family, coworkers, strangers ▪ Difficulty maintaining relationships (friends and romantic) ▪ <u>Feeling the need to jump out of your</u> skin when someone touches you, and even when used as a means to gesture when they say hello (includes family and friends) ▪ Avoiding hugs/handshakes from friends or family members ▪ Social Anxiety (negative feelings about themselves, and difficulty maintaining trusting relationships)

MEMORY PROBLEMS	▪ Short-Term ▪ Long-Term ▪ Loss of Time Difficulty remembering the events of the traumatic incident (it is very common remember fragments of memory)
ENGAGING IN ADDICTIVE TENDENCIES	▪ Abusing drugs, alcohol ▪ Anorexia / Bulimia (restricting, binging, purging)

AUTHOR'S
ANXIETY, FEARS, PHOBIAS, AND PTSD

My anxiety tends to intertwine with my fears, phobias, and Post-Traumatic Stress Disorder. As stated above, PTSD tends to affect people differently which is why I am willing to share some of my own issues and experiences in hopes that it will help others to understand that whatever it is that they may be going through, they are not alone. In addition, I hope that for friends, families, or even coworkers of someone who is suffering from anxiety, fears, phobias, and PTSD, that they will learn that these disorders can be a very frightening ordeal to live with and that 'they' should not label or make blind assumptions about these people. Characteristically, signs and symptoms can manifest in anyone who has ever been victimized, survived a tragic experience or been severely affected by other means that causes extreme emotional stress and anxiety attributing to reoccurring flashbacks, nightmares, and emotional distress. For some, the slightest trigger could cause them to relapse and relive the tragic event over and over in their mind.

However, the initial PTSD panic attack might not occur for days, weeks, months, or even years following the incident. Nevertheless, whenever a PTSD related panic attack does occur, the individual will likely feel as if they are re-experiencing the actual tragic event all over again but for the first time. Try to image that you have experienced the same nightmare several nights in a row with each night getting more terrifying by the next. Every night before you go to sleep, you find yourself feeling too distraught and terrified to close your eyes. Now, try to imagine that you do fall asleep and you find yourself feeling trapped and unable to wake up. Each night, you turn the volume up on the alarm clock but it doesn't help and you sleep through your alarm. With night terrors, they are technically a sleep disorder known as sleep terrors in which the person wakes up in a terrified state of mind. If you are like me, who almost always remembers my dreams in great detail, this only intensifies the waking up part. The problem is that when you do finally wake up from your terror-nightmare, you dread going back to sleep ever again which only leads to insomnia, increased anxiety, depression, emotional distress, and other psychological and physical problems.

For years, I had terrifying night terrors and I would experience them about 3-4 a month. One of the anxiety medications that I take is called, Atarax which does come in a generic form (Hydroxyzine Hydrochloride). I was prescribed the medication PRN (as needed) every 8-hours. Beginning back in July 2013, I began taking one dose every night before I went to sleep and it has reduced my night terrors from about 3-4 a month to maybe 1 or 2 every 2-3 months. Now, just because this medication helped with my night terrors, does not suggest that it will do the same for everyone. I would recommend talking with your doctor about Atarax or a similar anxiety medication. In addition to the Atarax, I have been taking Buspar (generic: Buspirone) two times a day since November 2012 and I also take Klonipin (generic: Clonazepam) as needed for panic attacks. Depending on the severity of your anxiety, fears, phobias, and PTSD, others may need one or more anxiety medications to help with their recovery but medications alone are not the key to recovery.

KNOWN TRIGGERS

Night terrors are just the tip of the iceberg because the thing about triggers is that they can take on many forms; from scents, to changes in temperatures, seeing/feeling objects, specific people, locations, words, etc. As for me, one of my known triggers is the word, 'suicide.' It does not matter if someone mentions the word, I see it in print form, or someone is talking about suicidal tendencies. This trigger word does not cause me to feel suicidal but it does trigger two very specific memories in my past when I lost my stepfather in 1997 and a former college roommate in 2003. Even though both incidents occurred years apart and were unrelated, the problem is that I suppressed all of my thoughts and emotions around the time of each incident and did not bother to talk to anyone about how I was feeling. Basically, I kept the emotions bottled up inside and managed to forget about it for many years – or so, I thought.

In August 1997, my stepfather committed suicide with a handgun to the head. Sure, I felt sadness for my mother and my stepbrother but for some reason I cannot seem to remember feeling anything for myself. It is not as if I am without empathy because anyone who knows me now or back then would say that I am a very loving person who would go out of my way to help others by finding ways to cheer them up. Yet, for years I felt emotionally numb inside when it came to Josh.

In May 2003, one of my former college roommates, committed suicide with a shotgun during finals week and once again, I buried my thoughts and emotions deep inside my mind and I guess, I just didn't let that incident trouble me. However, for years following the second incident, I constantly questioned my own mentality wondering why I did not see any signs that my college roommate was depressed. I was guilt ridden and convinced that I should have somehow noticed signs or symptoms based on my stepfather's suicide. I now know that no two suicides are the same. But for years, I was consumed with so much guilt and anxiety over both incidents because I felt like I should have been more observant to their behaviors. I tend to be a very observant person; after all, I have been a criminal investigator for over 12-years. Hence, I guess that I still question myself at times; why wasn't I more observant of their behaviors? Then again, perhaps, the aftermath of these two incidents is what has caused me to become a stronger and more observing person of others.

Around the time of the second suicide, I had been working on my Bachelor's Degree in Criminal Justice with an emphasis in Law Enforcement. In addition, for years I had been working in the criminal justice field without any awareness that I had been suffering from signs and symptoms of Post-Traumatic-Stress Disorder (PTSD). Honestly, I didn't even know what anxiety was back then. In fact, I wasn't diagnosed with PTSD until 2007 while I was working on my Master's Degree in Criminal Justice. Ever since I was a kid, all I ever wanted to be was a police officer. I had applied to several major police departments (LAPD, NYPD, Atlanta PD, Saint Louis County PD, and Saint Louis City PD). I tested in the top percentiles with the written and oral exams but it wasn't until the day that I took the Physical Agility Test (PT) for Saint Louis Metropolitan (City) Police Department that my life would change forever.

The test included a ¼ mile obstacle course with running, jumping, lifting/pulling/pushing weights, climbing, dragging a 150 pound dummy – and all of that was the easy part! Towards the end of the test I had to dry-fire a handgun six-times in each hand which I would have thought would have been a piece of cake but far from that. From the moment I squeezed the trigger, I felt frozen in time as if several hours had passed. Yet, I heard a soft voice in the back of my head which was actually the instructor yelling at the top of his voice; but all that I heard was a muffled sound. Apparently, the instructor was yelling that I only had a couple of minutes before the time would expire. Before I knew it, I was drenched in sweat despite the cold temperature inside the gymnasium.

As soon as I pulled that trigger and dry-fired the first shot, I felt like I was yanked out of the present and trapped somewhere in the past between 1997 and 2003 surrounding both suicides. All of a sudden, I felt like I was in the room when my stepfather and college roommate pulled the trigger, ending their lives even though I was miles away when each occurred. It was as if a flood gate had just opened up or a water dam had busted from some type of powerful explosion causing all of my bottled up emotions to pour out at once consuming my mind with uncontrollable anger and emotional distress. I felt trapped inside a shark infested fear-cage.

Even then, I had no idea what PTSD was or that I had experienced symptom of it which only increased over time. It is now, 2014 and nearly 16-years have passed since my stepfather shot himself and 11-years since my college roommate shot himself and yet even today, both incidents seems like they both occurred yesterday with every detail fresh in my mind. Who would have thought that an actual trigger from a gun would have been my initial PTSD trigger? To this day, my triggers are more managed thanks to my several anxiety medications, therapy sessions, meditation, church and prayer, positive coping skills, and good friends who I can turn to for help. Yes, I now know that there is no shame in asking for help.

But, the subject of suicides are not my only known triggers because the mere mention of guns, looking at guns in person, in print, on TV or in a movie can also trigger my PTSD episodes. When I was in-patient treatment for my anorexia and bulimia several years ago, I had two severe PTSD attacks, which is something that I will never forget! The first incident occurred when I met my roommate. When he took his shirt off, I noticed he had a dressing across the right side of his chest. I made the mistake of asking what happened. He attempted suicide and shot himself in his chest. Oh, perfect; talk about a double whammy for me! I probably should have just stopped him there but he went on talking about how he had been suicidal for months and then the next thing I remember he was describing the gun in details and what it felt like when the bullet hit his chest. Before I knew it, I was having a panic attack and consumed with nightmarish flashbacks in my mind about my stepfather and college roommate's suicides. Luckily, I was able to get to one the nurses and take one of my other anxiety medications, Klonipin which is a benzodiazepine in the same class as medications like Xanax, Valium, and Ativan. The nurse and I agreed that it might have been a good idea to switch roommates, which we did. One would think that with my PTSD related triggers to guns and suicides, they should have assigned me a different roommate.

The other event occurred during a group therapy session. The group was a dual-diagnosis therapy group. [Dual diagnosis is for anyone with a mental disorder who is/was addicted to drugs and/or alcohol. As of 2014, I have never experimented with drugs and I have been sober from alcohol for 12 ½ years]. The group therapy session was optional but I figured that the more groups I went to, the more proactive I was with my eating disorder recovery. Well, this group in particular had a therapist and one other patient (small group). Just my luck, the other patient had been suicidal and he kept talking about his fascination with guns. I asked him to change the subject and the therapist knew of my PTSD with guns and suicides. But, the 17-year old kid kept talking about guns and suicides. Thankfully, I could feel the anxiety coming on and I did the best thing for me at the time which was to leave the group. Granted, I still had a PTSD related anxiety attack but it wasn't by far one of the worst I've experienced in the past. Later, when the group ended, the kid walked up to me and apologized because he remembered that I had PTSD triggers related to guns and suicides.

Needless to say, my dream of being a police officer was nothing but a foreign memory to me, or at least one that I wish that I could forget! Nevertheless, I have always enjoyed watching TV shows like NCIS, NCIS: Los Angeles, Law & Order: SVU, actions movies like Die Hard and Bad Boys but, these days, I need to have on hand my Klonipin because the mere sight of guns or the sound of gunshots can trigger severe emotional distress for me. Fireworks during a Fourth of July celebration are no picnic for me either because the sounds tend to remind me of gunshots which triggers PTSD episodes. This year, the 4th was on a Friday and every Friday night I attend church. The pastor finished his sermon minutes before a firework event was to take place about 2 miles away at my local mall. I took a leap of faith and decided to watch the show with some of the church members at the edge of the church parking lot. Honestly, I did really well at first because the sounds were too far away for me to hear any noises. However, a couple of church members decided to bring out a multi-shooting firework noise maker from their cars and before I realized what was occurring, off went a 5 minute display of intense sounds of fireworks not more than maybe 10 feet from where I had been standing. With each snap, crackle, and pop, I thought for sure that someone was firing gun shots in the air. My heart began racing as I almost grabbed the arm of a nearby lady friend from church. Thankfully, I keep as supply of my Klonipin in a medicine container on my keychain. Between the Klonipin and silent screams to Jesus, I managed to calm myself down before any PTSD episodes occurred. That said, while it is important to know what your triggers are, it is also important to prepare yourself in the event that you cannot control or avoid every known trigger. I now know that some of my known triggers include any mention of guns, looking at guns, or the use of the word, 'suicide.' Flashbacks may seem like no big deal but frankly, they can be very traumatizing.

Personally, I have no thoughts of suicide when triggered by flashbacks of my stepfather and college roommates' suicides but rather I feel slingshot back to 1997 and 2003 as if I am reliving both incidents all over again for the first time. Even now, as I am writing this book, I can feel the anxiety pumping through my nerves as I am reminding myself to calm down and relax my mind and body while remaining grounded in the present rather than the past. These days, my level of anxiety does not always manifest into panic attacks or full blown PTSD related episodes as it once did, because now I have positive reinforcement tools to help desensitize any forethought emotions before any major anxiety comes about. This is why it is very important to learn what are your known triggers for anxiety, panic attacks, and (where it applies) PTSD episodes. Even if you are not aware of what are all of your known triggers, it is equally important to recognize any cues that your body may warn you of. For example, when I begin to feel anxious or on edge about something, I often feel a tingling and a light burning sensation in my forearms, followed by what feels like a drop in blood sugar, and then the feeling that my blood is warming up through my chest. If I do not pay attention to these cues, then yes; I am likely to experience a full onset panic attack or PTSD episode. I know most of my body's cues and because of this is why I am able to fight most of my flashbacks rather than losing control of my mind and body.

POST-TRAUMATIC STRESS DISORDER:
SEXUAL HARASSMENT-SEXUAL ASSAULT
LINDENWOOD UNIVERSITY

The two suicides are not the only triggers for my PTSD episodes. I truly believe that once a person has experienced Post-Traumatic Stress Disorder that they are predisposed to PTSD for other traumatic life events. In 2011, I was sexually harassed and assaulted multiple times by one of my gerontology professors in graduate school. At the time, I was working on my second master's degree which would have been in counseling towards my Licensed Professional

Counseling (LPC) certification. The incident occurred at Lindenwood University where I earned my first master's degree, in criminal justice administration. The 9-credit trimester cluster class was an elective course that met one night a week at the Westport campus in Maryland Heights, Missouri. The class had about 13-15 students which was the average class sizes for trimester clusters. The classroom was setup with side-by-side tables in a u-shape with students sitting along the outside perimeter of the tables and with the instructor's desk on the inside but about 10 ft. back. I was about 36 at the time of the incidents. I am presently 40-years old.

The First Incident

The instructor had just given the class a 15-minute break and while I do not remember exactly what I said at the time, apparently, it was an amusing comment because many of my classmates were laughing as they began to exit the classroom. The instructor walked towards me while laughing as well. I was still sitting in my chair as I was engaged in a conversation with a female classmate to my left. Before I had realized what occurred, the instructor stepped into my personal space with about an arms width of a table length between us, but that did not stop the instructor from reaching across the table with his left hand in a grabbing motion as he pinched my right cheek with his thumb, index and middle fingers. He squeezed and tugged in a way that can only be described as an older relative who squeezes the cheek of a child. He held on to my cheek in an upward/downward motion for mere seconds but it sure felt like hours had passed. I was so confused by what he did that I just froze rather than what I wish I had done instead – pushed him away while stepping back in a defensive pose! I felt so violated. To this day, I still replay the incident in my mind but with the thought process of; *Would have; Could have; Should have…*

Luckily, the female classmate who I had been talking with had witnessed the incident. I was ready to leave class early but at the same time, I was still in shock by the incident. The classmate said that I should report the instructor for assaulting me. After class, she offered to be a witness if I had decided to report the instructor to the department chair. The next day, I sent an email complaint to the department chair, who advised me that she would take care of the incident.

The Second Incident

For ***the second incident***, which occurred a couple of weeks later, the instructor asked me during class to stay after so that he could discuss the subject of my final project due weeks later. I thought for sure that he was planning to ask me about my complaint so I asked the same classmate to wait with me after class as a witness. Well, after class, the instructor told everyone they could leave but again reminded me to remain behind. My witness stood in the classroom waiting for me and naturally, the instructor asked her to wait outside the classroom so he could discuss my project in private. The door was in an opened position and as soon as my classmate exited the classroom, the instructor closed the door. He walked back over to where I was standing near his desk. I stood about 2-3 feet away from the instructor while facing him. We talked for about five minutes and I could not wait to get the hell out of there!

The thing about PTSD is that it is very common to have difficulty remembering many details of our traumatic experiences but instead, begin to remember fragments of the incident over time. Basically, with PTSD our mind can be comparable to that of Swiss cheese, with the holes as gaps in memory that causes us much emotional distress as we attempt to make sense of everything. While triggers tend to be very personal and different for everyone, they are also our body's way of attempting to make sense of what we once experienced. Some people experience physical memory ailments such as different degrees of anxiety to pains in the heart, muscles, stomach, etc., while others experience partial or complete memories in the forms of flashbacks and night terrors. Whether we remember partial or complete memories of our traumatic incidents, it is very common to re-experience detailed memories of the event.

I remember as clear as day that I was wearing a long-sleeve, three buttoned collared shirt tucked out of my blue jeans. My backpack was hanging over my right shoulder. I also remember that the instructor kept inching closer towards me and one would think I would have backed up but I just stood there, frozen. Out of nowhere, the instructor reached out with his left arm and stepped inside my personal bubble which was way too close for comfort. We were probably ½ foot apart and yet I didn't step back. To this day, I still can't believe I did not back away or say anything to him at the time.

Out of the corner of my eye, I remember watching as he swayed closer towards me and then, as he reached out towards my right shoulder with his left hand and I just stood there, confused and defenseless. In the moment, I just stood there, frozen as if his movements appeared to be in slow motion. I felt powerless to do anything which for me was out of the ordinary because at the time I had been working in Loss Prevention, arresting shoplifters. I had about 12-years' experience in loss prevention and I was used to people threatening to inflict bodily harm and it never really bothered me because I knew how to defend myself if needed and yet, with this incident, I felt powerless to do anything as my instructor leaned in closer towards me. The next thing I knew, he grabbed my shirt collar and appeared to adjust it while gliding his hand across my shoulder as if to massage my neck and shoulder. This was followed by the instructor telling me how he had wanted to adjust my collar all night because it was uneven. Perhaps, he could have just said something to me during the 3-hour class period that my collar needed adjusted and *I* could have adjusted it. About a week later, I reported the second incident to the department chair. Once again, she said that she would take care of it.

The Third Incident

For *the third incident*, which occurred on the last night of class; there was a horrible ice storm and many of my classmates had hoped that the class would end early due to the inclement weather. For this class, each of us had to present a PowerPoint presentation of our final project. There were two students before me who had completed their presentation and when it came down to my presentation, I was about 5 minutes into it when the instructor received a phone call. He advised me to continue with my project while he stepped into the hallway to talk on his phone. He was out of the classroom for about ten minutes when the rest of the class was like, *"Josh, you are done."* Technically, our projects were supposed to be about 20-25 minutes but due to the severe weather conditions, I happily agreed that I finished my presentation early. When the instructor returned to the classroom, he advised everyone that he was dismissing the class 2 hours early due to the weather. He stated to the class that for those who did not complete their presentation, not to worry because he would adjust the grades on a curve and that *by not doing their projects it would not affect their grades.*

As I was exiting the classroom with the other students, the instructor said, *"Josh, wait a minute, if you or any of your classmates wish to stay the night at my home, you (notice how he said, 'you' and 'Josh' and not 'they') are welcome to stay the night at my home; you are more than welcome to."* Needless to say, everyone declined. I was so happy to be free from further incidents by this instructor; or so I would have thought.

About a week later, I received an email from the instructor. He asked if I still wanted to complete my PowerPoint presentation to receive full credit. I asked about the curve that he mentioned to the class. The instructor ignored my question but instead offered for me to make arrangements with him to go over to his home for a one-on-one presentation. He even offered to cook a meal. I respectfully declined and stated that I did not feel comfortable. At which point, the instructor offered to meet me at a Denny's and once again, I respectfully declined. He continued to send me email after email and he even left a couple of voice mails suggesting that I make arrangements to present my presentation or else my grade would reflect poorly for not completing the presentation. I offered to send him a copy of my presentation but he stated that it needed to be in person.

At the time, I had saved all of my emails and phone logs from the instructor. I emailed several of my former classmates who were not able to do their presentations on the last night of class due to the weather and asked them if the instructor had emailed or called them to make similar arrangements and yet; every single person I talked with stated that not only did the instructor not contact them but he gave them all "A"s for their presentation even though they did not actually present or send the instructor a copy of the presentation. I received a "C" for my presentation and an "F" for my final paper.

FORMAL COMPLAINT

It was at this time that I contacted the Dean of Faculty and Dean of Students and lodged a formal complaint for sexual harassment and assault against the instructor. If there is one thing that I am really good at doing, it is keeping phone logs and email records, as well as voice mail recordings of any corresponding communications. I emailed the deans a copy of the email communications with the date and time stamps, along with my phone records. About a week later, I met with the Dean of Faculty and Dean of Students in the Dean of Faculty's office. One by one, the Dean of Faculty addressed each of my complaints but sadly he had an excuse for each.

For the incident where the instructor pinched/squeezed my cheek, the Dean of Faculty stated that was merely something that his generation viewed as innocent playful touching and if the instructor did not perceive it to be sexual harassment, then it was not. I attempted to argue the incident further but the Dean refused to listen to any reasoning. When I stated that I perceived it as an assault, the Dean of Faculty basically stated that it was a two way streak and even as a third and impartial party *(impartial???)*, neither the instructor nor the dean interpreted it as an assault. At which point, the dean moved on two the second incident with the rubbing of my shoulder/shirt collar.

First, the Dean stated that I should have said something to the instructor directly rather than 'whining' to the department chair. Next, I was given the following example by the Dean of Faculty. *He went on to say how he has a dear friend who is an attorney and that one day he approached his friend to adjust his tie because it was crooked. At first, his friend took a step back (which is what I should have done) and then he said something to the Dean about how he could do it himself and that is what I should have said to the instructor.* The Dean also reiterated that I should have said something directly to the instructor rather than crying foul to the department chair about such nonsense.

As far as the rubbing of my shoulders, the Dean stated that it was a bit far-fetched because it would only be considered a sexual assault *if* he rubbed the shoulders of a female student. The Dean made it very clear that I should have said something directly to the instructor or else it was not sexual harassment. I asked if this was a Lindenwood policy and the Dean stated that was the law. I advised the Dean that he was incorrect because in my role as a loss prevention officer (retail law enforcement), I had conducted several training classes on sexual harassment and that most companies have policies in place; specifically stating that victims of sexual harassment are not required to confront their assailant directly because often this can cause a backlash against all involved. Furthermore, I explained that in the event that an employee does not feel comfortable approaching the person who has sexually harassed them, then they can go to the person's supervisor or another supervisor or human resources, especially where quid pro quo may be a factor (such as the incident with the instructor giving me a low grade for refusing to go to his home for a private one-on-one session to do my presentation).

The Dean of Faculty advised that I was incorrect and that he did not want to hear any more of my baseless accusations. In fact, the Dean went on to advised me that the instructor was previously married to a woman (I think he is a widower) and has children therefore he could not have done any of the things I had accused him of. I stated that I am heterosexual and I did not appreciate a male instructor doing what he did. The Dean replied back, "He didn't do anything that you are claiming he did because he is not gay!" I attempted to dispute the dean's blind justifications but he stated that was the end of that alleged incident and then he moved on to the next incident.

As far as the instructor's invitation for me to go over to his home for a private one-on-one session to present my PowerPoint presentation, the Dean of Students finally spoke up and made the following statement, *"Typically, we do not invite the students over to an instructor's home for liability reasons."* I thought to myself, *"Wow; that actually made the first bit of sense."* I just assumed that if other students were to make similar allegations about an instructor's actions that it would come down to a game of he/she/said (regardless of gender or sexual orientation). However, the Dean of Students has a completely different take on the word '*liability*'.

The Dean went on to say that if a student were to get into a car accident on the way to/from the instructor's home, then there could be a liability issue. Unreal! Naturally, the Dean of Faculty had to chime in as well and he stated that I should not have made the suggestion to go over to the instructor's home in the first place. Say what? I stated that it was the instructor who made the suggestion and I was the one who declined *his* offer but the Dean dismissed my claims stating that I had no proof. I was dumbfounded. I asked both Deans if they had received my email attachments to my complaint, with the emails and phone records between the instructor and me. The Dean of Faculty concluded that I altered the emails and doctored the phone records to appear as if the instructor called me several times when he did not. I offered to use the Dean's computer to access my phone records with the proof but the Dean of Faculty declined.

Nevertheless, I asked the Dean of Faculty to explain why I received a "C" for my final presentation when every single one of my classmates had received an "A?" The Dean stated that it was not his place to change the grades of one of his instructors. When I asked about the "F" on my final paper, the Dean stated that it was the worst paper he had ever read by a student in all his years. I stated that I had asked a former instructor from an English course to read and evaluate it, and they said it would have probably received a solid "B." The Dean laughed.

Afterwards, I advised both Deans that these allegations were classic examples of sexual harassment including the instructor's quid-pro-quo in receiving lower grades for refusing his sexual advances. Once again, the Dean of Faculty reminded me that the instructor was married to a woman, had kids, and that because I did not ask the instructor to stop his alleged advances that there was no sexual harassment or assault. The Dean also stated that I used poor judgment by going to the department chair. It probably did not help that the Dean was about eighty years old and had an old-school way of looking at things like refusing to see that a male instructor could in fact sexually harass and assault a male student. Needless to say, I transferred schools but sadly only 9 of my 47 credits would transfer.

ZONES OF PERSONAL SPACE

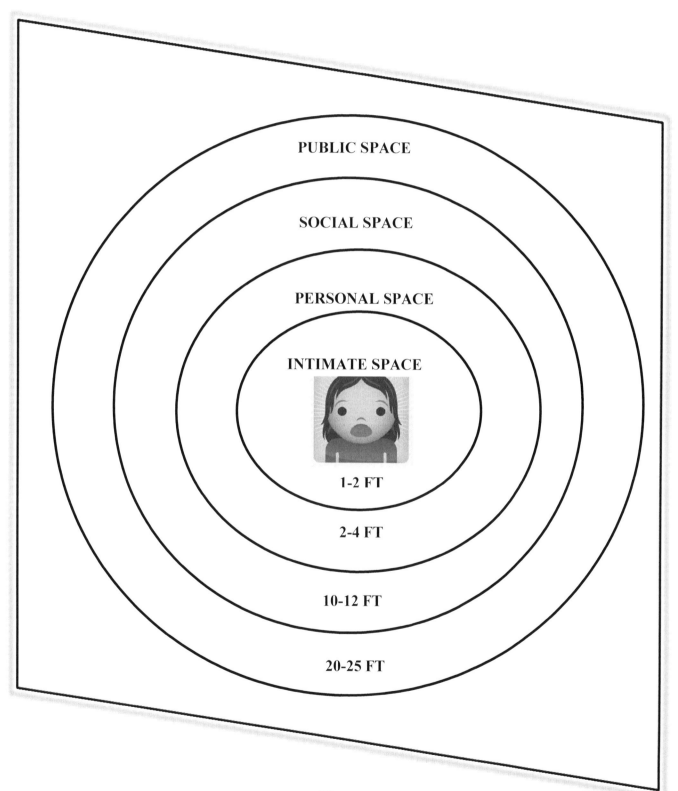

PUBLIC SPACE

SOCIAL SPACE

PERSONAL SPACE

INTIMATE SPACE

1-2 FT

2-4 FT

10-12 FT

20-25 FT

PTSD TRIGGERS

Post-Traumatic Stress Disorders can manifest whether or not victims gets justice for their victimization. With my incident, the school buried it as if nothing illegal occurred when in fact it did. I contacted about a dozen lawyers but none wanted to take my case. In cases where victims do report their victimization, many are unable to find prosecutors willing to prosecute even though a jury could have convicted the perpetrator. While others who are able to prosecute, there are some jurors with the same old school mentality as the Dean of Faculty who do not believe that a male can be a victim and more than a female can be a perpetrator, leading to an acquittal.

Unfortunately, the system isn't perfect and consequently victims can still develop PTSD regardless of whether they got justice for their victimization. For some, justice could simply be that their assailant gets terminated from their job, has to register as a sex offender, has to make a public apology, etc. Regardless of the outcome, nothing can undo the victimization but we can learn to recover from it and rise up as survivors. We need to believe in better things and distant our mind from negative things. After all, worrying about the bad things that happened might not prevent it from happening again but what it will do is keep us from enjoying the good things in life.

For me, I have problems with personal space and boundaries. I have friends and family members who approach me and want a give a hug or a handshake and from the moment that I see their arms coming towards me, I feel so much anxiety that at times I tend to experience flashbacks to my sexual assaults. I attend a church where everyone is very friendly and it is quite common to give handshakes, hugs, or to walk up to someone and place hands on someone's shoulder while saying, "*Hello*." When this happens to me, I typically want to jump about 3 feet out of my skin! Furthermore, romantic and social relationships can be very difficult revert away from isolation, for someone who has been a victim to sexual assault or abuse.

PTSD PANIC ATTACKS

When I have a PTSD related panic attack, my body feels motionless and trapped inside a fear-cage. I have chills yet my blood feels like it is boiling throughout my entire body. My anxiety feels like I am having a heart attack or stroke with my blood pressure upwards of 155/110. My friends have said that I look like I am in some type of trance as I am experiencing flashbacks of the traumatic events like they are in a constant loop in my mind. When my PTSD panic attack has passed, the actual attack typically lasts for about 30 seconds to a couple of minutes but I typically loose time and rather than minutes, I tend to feel as if hours have passed.

The following symptoms are commonly associated with PTSD related Panic Attacks:

- ➤ Tremors, shaking
- ➤ Vertigo, dizziness
- ➤ Chest pains, tightness
- ➤ Feeling like you are dying
- ➤ Gasping for air, hyperventilation
- ➤ Feeling like you are choking or suffocating
- ➤ Racing pulse, heart palpitations, irregular heart beats
- ➤ Feeling like you are watching a movie in your mind with the same scene repeated

F E A R S

-&-

P H O B I A S

AQUAPHOBIA

Moment of honesty here; I am absolutely terrified of the water whether it's in swimming pools, lakes, rivers, oceans, ponds, etc. I used to live in Tampa, Florida (1999-2000). One day, I went to the St. Petersburg (St. Pete) beach with some friends. At the time, I had a slight fear of the ocean after growing up on movies like Jaws and Piranha; so I was already a bit apprehensive when I was told by my friends that I had to actually go in the water rather than just lay on the sand. Needless to say that, the first time I went into the ocean was also my last! My friend, Jaime and I had large cups and had planned to catch small fish in the ocean to help take my mind off of my other fears such as sharks, octopus, and anything else large enough to put me out of my misery from ocean. But, I will never forget what happened on that rather eventful afternoon when catching small fish was the least of my concerns.

As soon as I walked into the ocean, Jamie stated that I needed to do the 'St. Pete shuffle.' I was like, "Huh?" She said that I would need to flap my feet up and downward (flutter) to scare away the stingrays. That didn't exactly help my fears any less. Well, the sand was brownish-yellow and I could see the sand under the water as we walked out to about waist high. I figured that all stingrays were a blackish color and I did not realize that the ones commonly found around this beach were also a tannish color similar to the sand. As soon as I heard what and why we had to do the shuffle, I was like, "I'm out of here!" But, my friend basically called me a chicken a dared me to stay where I was – which I reluctantly did. We were out there for about 15-20 minutes when she said, "Something just touched my leg." At first, I just froze and then I had Star Wars flashbacks to Episode IV when Luke, Chewy, Han, and Leah were trapped in the trash compactor and Luke made the comment, "Something just touched my leg;" and naturally as Han tells Luke that is just his imagination, out of nowhere, a snake like creature grabs a hold of Luke and pulls him under the sewage water. Nonetheless, after my minor stroll down memory lane, I just figured that Jaime was messing with me, or so I thought.

Not more than about a minute later, a woman about 20 ft. away screamed out that she just got stung by a stingray. Well, I don't know about her but I am quite sure that I swam to the beach before she did. There was no looking back as I practically kissed the sandy ground. Apparently, some species of stingrays' spines breakoff similar to stingers on many species of bees because I seem to remember that is exactly what happened to this woman as the lifeguards went into full Baywatch Rescue Mode. Honestly, between Jaime's comments and the woman's screams and my compounded fear of the water already, the rest is a blur, but the anxiety is still there every time I even stepped into a swimming pool. As weeks passed, whenever my friends wanted to go back to the beach, I happily declined. Of course, it did not help my fear levels anymore when that season, the local news stations had been reporting one shark attack after another at the very location where my incident occurred.

To this day, I do not go on float trips out of fear of alligators in the rivers and I do not go swimming in lakes out of fear of the unknown. Now, given; with a swimming pool, I can clearly see the bottom of the pool even in say 10-15 feet of water, yet there is something in my mind telling me otherwise. Whenever I go swimming in a pool that exceeds any depth in which I cannot stand up without my head above the water, I will typically swim ½ lengths of the pool. As soon as I approach the deep end, I fearfully turn around and swim back to the edge of the shallow end. Now, I do not typically have a panic attack if I am sitting on a pool deck near the deep water but there is some degree of anxiety nonetheless. This anxiety tends to increases if I am in the water at the edge of the deep end just about where the pool floor begins to decline. The irony is that while I am terrified of the oceans, I love boats just not the water. What is even more ironic, when I mediate, I often use the sounds of waves in the oceans because I tend to find it relaxing – as long as I am not physically there!

CLAUSTROPHOBIA

Another fear I have is confined spaces especially when it comes to elevators. If need be, I will walk up 30 flights of steps to avoid getting inside one of those boxed-in-for-dear-life-contraptions. In 2003, I was trapped inside an elevator at a JC Penney's where I was employed. This elevator was notorious for getting stuck and in the event that a customer would get trapped in the elevator, we would immediately call EMS and the fire department if we could not pry opens the doors in a timely manner. Of course, this did not apply to employees; so naturally when I got stuck between floors with the doors opened about a ½ foot apart, the store manager did not feel that it was cost effective to call EMS and the fire department or to even allow managers to attempt to pry open the doors with the off chance that the doors could break and then be costly to repair.

I remember it was on a Sunday and the store manager was off property and even though the fire department and EMS were called because I was beginning to freak out inside the box, the manager on duty stated that she talked with the store manager and he felt it would be more cost effective to wait for the elevator repairman to show up and let me out. Prior to that incident, I was not claustrophobic but I seem to remember the sensation that the air was thinning and I felt like the walls were closing in on me even though I could barely get my arm through the small opening between the doors as the firemen and EMT attempted to talk me down. I was trapped inside that metal box for about 3 freaking hours! Apparently, the store manager and the manager on duty were attempting to compute the cost of an elevator repairman on a Sunday which would have been either 1.5 or 2x the cost. I mean, all the firemen needed to do, was to use their axe and pry open the doors as they had in the past for customers. Apparently, there would have been more priority had I been a pregnant employee – good to know the store manager had his ducks in a row!

I remember the firemen urging the store manager to allow them to pry open the doors but the store manager would not authorize it. After about 30 minutes of that B.S., the store manager made the decision to wait for the elevator repairman to let me out with his special key. Apparently, the one elevator repairman on-call was at a family picnic so we had to wait for him to wrap things up which oddly took about 2 hours after several calls between him and the store manager of how he was on his way. So, the best part was when the repairman said he could not figure out why the doors were stuck and after about 20 minutes of him monkeying around, a fireman FINALLY pried open the dam doors! What a nightmare!

After the incident, I remember that for the first few months I felt claustrophobic in the strangest places like parking garages and crowds. If there was a car stopped in front and behind my vehicle while waiting to find a parking place in a parking garage and me with no place to go due to the cars parked along my sides, I felt like I was holding my breath under water the entire time. Eleven years later and to this day, I try to avoid elevators as much as possible but it doesn't mean that I can never get inside an elevator again because there are some places like federal buildings where stairs are only for emergencies. I do avoid airplanes because I feel trapped and honestly, I cannot remember the last time I even flew. I prefer to travel by Amtrak because if need be, I can move from one car to another. But, thanks to my anxiety medications, therapy, meditations, prayer, and my positive coping skills, many of my known phobias are a bit more manageable these days.

COPING

The things we dwell on eventually becomes our realities but if we learn to effectively handle our anxieties and phobias as they come about, we will ultimately reshape the way we view things. Personally, I would rather feel happy than to allow any negative things to spoil the good things I have to enjoy. Now, I'm not going to lie and sell you some fantasize about how I have been cured from my anxieties, fears, phobias or PTSD attacks because there is no magic cure; but we can learn to manage our triggers more effectively so that each incident is less fearful and more carefree. Audrey Hepburn once said that nothing is impossible because the word 'IMPOSSIBLE' clearly states that "I'm Possible!" Life isn't meant to be easy all the time; sometimes we have our ups and downs; our bad and our good; but our past does not define us, it only makes us stronger.

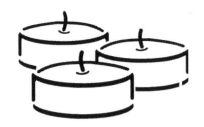

POSITIVE COPING SKILLS

AROMA THERAPY is a holistic form of medicine that uses minerals from plants, vitamins and scented oils, creams, lotions, and candles for the sole purpose of relaxing the person's mind, mood, and perceptions. The main focus of Aroma Therapy is for therapeutic purposes. Aroma Therapy can be used by breathing in different scented fragrances that may include the use of mist humidifiers or candle incense burners. Other forms of Aroma Therapy include topical agents in the use of massages, calming of the skin and pores, or for soaking in baths.

BIOFEEDBACK THERAPY is a learned behavior in binding the power of one's mind through awareness and the ability to take back control of one's overall health. Biofeedback promotes stress release and the ability to relax the body from head to toe. During treatment, painless electrodes are attached to the fingers and head which send signals to a wave monitor that displays images and flashes of lights to illustrate blood pressure, skin temperature, and muscle activities. I remember doing Biofeedback therapy when I was an adolescent. The electrodes were attached to my fingers and my body's core temperature would typically begin around 60 $^{\circ F}$ and in the background a tape played of a man's voice in the form of meditative speech (today, some therapists use isotones that target specific levels of brainwaves, mediation CD's or sound machines). From what I remember, I needed to relax my mind and body to where I no longer felt chilled or anxious but instead warm and relaxed. The wavelength machine would interpret my body's core temperature change. When I was really relaxed, my core temperature went upwards of 80s. Of course, at that time in my life, I had not yet experienced any of the physical traumas that affected me later in life; nor did I have any clue what PTSD was back then. At the time, biofeedback was just a therapeutic treatment that I used to help relax.

EYE MOVEMENT DESENSITIZATION AND REPROCESSING (EMDR) is a type of psychotherapy that was specifically created to help those with severe PTSD. This type of therapy should only be conducted by a trained therapist who has been certified in EMDR Therapy. EMDR is said to help with any unresolved memories of traumatic experiences. This process can take anywhere from eight to thirteen weeks minimum over the course of an 8-steps program in which the person learns how to safely (in a controlled environment) recall any distressing images through a series of bilateral sensory inputs and side-by-side eye movements that is similar to rapid eye movement (REM); however the person remains in Alpha and Beta waves. EMDR therapy requires a clinical therapist who has been certified in EMDR therapy and should not be conducted by any clinical therapist not certified in EMDR therapy. Personally, I have not attempted EMDR therapy because my clinical therapist is not certified in this type of therapy; however, EMDR is known for helping people with emotional distress. For additional information, please visit www.EMDR.com.

EXERCISING (AEROBIC & ANAEROBIC) is an excellent source for fighting anxiety but I strongly urge you to be very careful that your heart rate does not fall too low or skyrocket too high. After all, you do not want to push yourself from one extreme to the next. Riding a bike in the fresh air or running in the cool air, or swimming are great types of exercises to help reduce anxiety. Walking in a swimming pool is also recommended. Exercising as a coping skill can be an effective way of allowing your mind to fixate on things like your overall health rather than any specific limitations. If you feel like any of these types of exercise may be too difficult for you, then take it slow at first and go for a brisk walk. Personally, for years I avoided exercising because I was do depressed and filled with anxiety that I just felt blah inside; however, since I have joined a gym and have engaged in different types of exercises on a daily basis, my anxiety, stress levels, and depression have declined greatly. I also recommend working with a certified trainer, nutritionist, or dietitian to help transform your mind as well as your body's physical fitness.

HOLISTIC THERAPY is a way of relaxing the physical, mental, emotional, and spiritual elements of a person's health. Holistic *Medicine* uses the approach of treating the whole body rather than healing specific elements. Holistic medicine typically includes lifestyle changes that may include diet and exercise, vitamins and herbs, acupuncture and aroma therapy. Unfortunately, there are some negative types of Holistic Medicine which include diet restriction, juicing, and colon cleansing with the use of laxatives. If you are suffer from anorexia or bulimia, diet restriction and cleansings are not the best type of treatments for you. I am recovered from nearly 30-years of anorexia and 10-years of bulimia so this statement is based on my own knowledge of eating disorders. I also manage dozens of support groups in Facebook which includes those with eating disorders. If you suffer from eating disorders, I do not recommend any type of Holistic approaches that involves cleansings, juicing, restrictions, bingers, or the use of laxatives. *Acupuncture is a Chinese approach to therapy through the stimulation of specific parts of the body by inserting partial needles in the tip of the skin in which heat and pressure is used to alleviate stress and anxiety.* Personally, I have not used this technique but I have heard great things about this type of therapeutic coping skill. Some people believe that Acupuncture can substitute for chemotherapy and in lieu of other medical procedures to radiate the body of diseases.

HYPNOSIS THERAPY is typically a guided type of relaxation by a trained therapist certified as a hypnotist who can help people to achieve a heightened state of awareness. However, people have been known to tap into this heightened state of awareness through self-hypnosis and mediation. Nevertheless, for those just starting out with hypnosis, I strongly urged them to do so under the care of a licensed hypnotherapist. However, if looking for an economical approach, these days people can engage is self-hypnosis by listening to relaxation and meditation CDs or by downloading a phone application in the Android store or by visiting YouTube and searching for different types of meditation videos. If you suffer from a psychiatric disorder or if you take prescription medications for hypertension, depression, anxiety, etc., I strongly urge you to discuss the use of meditation programs that sends out specific Alpha, Beta, Delta, and Theta brainwaves which could affect dopamine and serotonin levels.

While increased serotonin levels promote healthy lifestyles and can reduce thoughts of depression, stress, and anxiety, too much release can actually lead to deadly consequences, known as **Serotonin Syndrome**. According to the Mayo Clinic, high levels of serotonin can cause the body to feel the effects of a drug or chemical overdose in which the body can feel severe symptoms of shivering with cold and hot flashes, diarrhea, tremors, seizures, and increased anxiety with panic attack sensations. If untreated, this can lead to death. About 2 years ago, I was diagnosed with Serotonin Syndrome following an emergency call to my psychiatrist in the middle of the night, who strongly urged me to go to the ER which I did. As it turned out, I was taking cough medicine that contained *dextromethorphan* which apparently acted like an antidote to one of my anxiety medications (Buspar) and antidepressant (Pristiq) and as a result of taking the cough medicine every 4-6 hours as directed, for about 4 days for bronchitis, it was as if I had stopped taking the Buspar (which I take 2 times a day) and the Pristiq (once per day). I experienced increased anxiety with thoughts of suicide, hot and cold flashes, and multiple panic attacks. While my diagnosis was not based on any type of mediation or hypnotic therapy, Serotonin Syndrome is scary nonetheless regardless of how it comes about. Basically, I experienced withdraw symptoms from the Buspar and the Pristiq. The ER physician said they diagnosed it quickly before it got worse. I was treated with higher doses of Klonipin (a Benzodiazepine anxiety medication that I take as needed), and I had to increase my Pristiq from 50 mg. to 100 for about a week and naturally, I had to stop taking the cough medicine. Let this incident be a warning to those who take anxiety and antidepressant medications, to check with your doctor and/or pharmacist when combining with over the counter (OTC) medications. Some medications and types of meditation practices can lead to increased levels of serotonin and dopamine levels. Please use caution when engaging in any type of approach that may affect these levels.

BRAINWAVE FREQUENCY CHART

BETA	Active, nervous, restless thinking, active concentration
ALPHA	Relaxed state of mind, awake
THETA	Dream state, deep meditation, hypnosis; rapid eye movement (REM) occurs
DELTA	Deep dreamless sleep

DISCLAIMER:

[NEVER ATTEMPT ANY RELAXATION TECHNIQUES WHILE OPERATING A MOTOR VEHICLE OR EQUPMENT REQUIRING CONCENTRATION.]

MINDFUL RELAXATION THERAPY includes a combination of treatments from deep breathing exercise to guided imagery, mindfulness meditation, and progressive muscle relaxation.

- *Deep Breathing* exercises involve learning to breathe from your abdomen instead of your chest. When taking in deep breaths, your abdomen expands and when you release your breath, your abdomen contracts inward. At the same time, when you breathe in, your eyes are closed as you breathe in through your nose and exhale through your mouth. However, it is very easy to hyperventilate if not done properly. Do not overdue this exercise or push beyond your limits. Listen to your body. The idea here is to help the mind and body, not weaken it.

- *Guided Imagery* is a means of concentrating on specific images, colors, or textures by learning to focus on it in your mind; by learning to let go of any negative fixations and then relax both the mind and body. The idea is to find the ability to put aside all of the negative images we tend to criticize ourselves over on a daily basis and then learn to replace it with joyful images in order to achieve a peaceful wellbeing state of mind.

- *Mindfulness Meditation* is used to help clear one's mind of negative thoughts and emotions. It is a learned behavior in grounding yourself to release any negativity. The following is a mindful meditation exercise that I have used for years that has helped when I am anxious or stressed:

  1. *Sit in a chair with your feet planted flat on the ground. Sit up with your back firmly aligned with the back of the chair and with your hands resting on your legs or in my lap.*

40

2. *Close your eyes and imagine that you are a tree with your feet as the roots planted in the ground beneath you.*

3. *For the next 3-5 minutes, try to think of whatever it is that has been bothering you.*

4. *Next, try to imagine that all of your negative thoughts and emotions are slowly cleansing from your body, down through your veins; from your head down your legs with your arms as limbs and your feet as the trunk.*

5. *Next, imagine that the roots of your feet are digging deeper down through the ground to the center of the earth pulling away from you any old and wilted branches of negativity as clouds begin to spout water over you, washing away any other negative emotions into the ground beneath your roots.*

6. *Next, begin to feel the rays of the bright sun as it touches your face causing you to sprout out colorful leaves from your limbs fed by joyful and positive emotions. As you continue with your deep breathing exercise, once again, sit up tall with body feeling rejuvenated and the tree like form feeling freshly planted and blooming with joy.*

7. *Next, take a deep breath in through your nose and out through your mouth and rise up from the ground with yours arms raised above your head in a stretch of your arms while taking in your relaxed state of mind as you feel all negativity purged from your mind and body.*

- ***Progressive Muscle Relaxation*** is a way of tightening the muscles in your arms and hands, legs and feet and then immediately relaxing each muscle group one at a time. However, be careful with this technique as it can also lead to painful muscle cramps if you push yourself too hard.

YOGA AND MEDITATION THERAPIES are great ways of healing both your body and mind of anxiety, fears, phobias, and PTSD. It will take practice to cleanse your body of all negativity but if you keep working at it, you will be able to reduce a great deal of those stressors in no time. The nice thing about yoga and meditation exercises is that they can include mindfulness mediation and self-hypnosis techniques as a way of clearing your mind of any negative thoughts and emotions. You will learn to bring balance to your body and mind. Yoga and meditation therapy can be performed in a group or solo setting. Between, Netflix, smart phones and smart televisions, Android applications, DVDs and YouTube downloads, Yoga and Meditation can be conducted virtually any time and place.

TV SHOWS & MOVIES

If you are still struggling with finding ways to cleanse your mind and body of those pesky anxieties, fears, phobias, or PTSD panic attacks, I recommend changing your environment by taking a break from current mindset. Try watching one of your favorite TV shows but more specifically; try watching a comedy or uplifting show that will not trigger any of your issues. The basic idea here is to snap your mind out of its current state of mind. As for me, I typically watch rerun episodes of the 1980's comedy show, ALF. What can I say but for me, it keeps me laughing. While I love to watch reruns of NCIS, NCIS: Los Angeles, and Law & Order: SVU, not an episode goes by where there isn't some type of shot fired or the sight of guns, which sadly triggers my anxiety levels instead of my 'uplifting' levels. If not ALF, then I like to watch rerun episodes of Highway to Heaven or Touch by an Angel.

PRAYER & FAITH

If you are a Christian like I am, try watching a Christian related movie about God or some type of inspirational show or read the bible and meditate on the word. You could always try praying to God or whoever is your higher power. HE is always with you and you do not need to go far to find HIM. He only wants you to ask for his help. If God brings you to it, HE will bring you through it. All you need to do is ask.

"Be careful for nothing; but in everything by prayer and supplication with thanksgiving let your requests be made known until God. And the peace of God, which passes all understanding, shall keep your hearts and minds through Christ Jesus."
--- Philippians 4:6-7

"I can do all things through Christ who strengthens me."
--- Philippians 4:13

"I shall call upon HIM, and he will answer me; He will be with me in trouble; He will deliver me and I will honor him with long life. I will satisfy Him, and show HIM my salvation."
--- Psalm 91: 15-16

"Many are the afflictions of the righteous, but the Lord delivers him of them all."
-- Psalm 34:19

MUSIC THERAPY

Music therapy is a great way of releasing anxiety and stress as well as helping to change our mood from depressed, anxious, fearful, etc. Between the radio, CD players, and even mp3 players in our automobiles, access to the internet through smart phones and smart televisions, Android and IPhone markets, we have the ability to engage in this type of therapy virtually any time and place. If you prefer CDs, then I recommend keeping some of your favorite CDs in your automobile or particular songs downloaded on your devices so that you can listen to them at a moment's notice. I recommend listening to a song and then writing down a reflection of how the song made you feel. I strongly believe in positive coping skills. I work with a wide range of groups in Facebook through support groups, for victims and survivors of sexual violence, domestic violence and intimate partner violence (IPV), child abuse, bullying, anorexia, bulimia, PTSD and anxiety and a Music Therapy group for everyone and the feedback has been very positive. I work with people who have been through the kind of things in life that nobody should ever have to experience but they respond very well to music therapy. Every week, I add a new song and ask that people talk about how the song made them feel so that others would know that they are not alone with their victimization. Of course, you don't need to be a victim to do Music Therapy because whether words or instrumental, music itself has a way of affecting one's mood.

ART THERAPY

Art therapy is also another great coping skill, especially for children who have difficulty expressing in words how they feel. You don't need to be a great artist to express how you feel. If you can only draw stick figures, then so be it—but at least, you are finding ways of externalizing your thoughts and emotions. Are therapy includes drawings, paintings, sculptures; the use of crayons, markers, pencils, paint, clay, etc. Art therapy has endless capabilities

DISCLAIMER II

While it is never a good idea to keep your thoughts and emotions bottled up inside, many therapists recommend journaling as a positive outlet for externalizing these thoughts and emotions; however, not everyone is able to write about how and why they feel the way they do. The following exercises and questions are designed to help those with anxiety, fears, phobia, and

PTSD as a means of exploring ways of talking about their thoughts and emotions in the form of a journal or diary format.

It is important to remember that with any form of therapeutic techniques, people may experience some level of anxiety, depression, sadness, or even joy and happiness in the early stages of their recovery process. Regardless, you should feel be very proud of yourself for attempting to do any of these exercises because this is a survivor mentality. You have to want to recover in order to feel recovered.

The intent of these exercises is intended to be helpful and not harmful to your health. If you feel like a particular section or a particular question is too emotionally painful to answer then by all means feel free to skip it or return to that section at a later time. If you are under the care of a therapist, I strongly recommend that you discuss whether these exercises and questions would be helpful or emotionally detrimental to your recovery process. You may wish to bring this workbook with you to your therapy sessions to discuss your responses with your therapist.

There is no right or wrong answers to any of these questions and exercises. You may wish to respond to the same sets of questions about 6 months later to see if any of your responses have changed.

RECOVERY EXERCISES:
GETTING TO KNOW '*ME*' ALL OVER AGAIN

Section I: Memory Teasers

Note: Some of these questions might seem a bit odd but one thing to remember is that with PTSD people tend to have memory problems and difficulty concentrating. It is quite common for someone to forget something as simple as their own date of birth or even what the current month is.

1. My first and middle name is

_____

2. Today's date is:

Month _____   Day _____   Year _____

I had to think about it for more than a minute: _____ Yes _____ No

3. Do I have any nicknames that other people like to call me? If so, what are these names and how does it make me feel?

_____

_____

4. I was born in this month?

_____

5. The year I was born was _____ and there is something very significant about this year to me; because:

_____

_____

6. I feel relaxed when I

_____

_____

7. My hobbies include

_____

_____

_____

8. My eye color is _____ but if I could change the colors of my eyes, they would be _____ because:

_____

_____

9. The length of my hair is (bald, short, shoulder length, long, other: _____). If I could magically change the length of my hair, it would be (bald, short, shoulder length, long, other: _____); because:

10. I describe my physical appearance as:

_____

_____

11. I am currently experiencing the following emotions:

_____   _____   _____

12. I wish I was experiencing the following emotions instead:

_____   _____   _____

13. My favorite color is:

_____

14. I would rather (√): _____ walk _____ jog _____ run _____ drive

15. I have this many tattoos _____ and they have the following meaning: (or) I do not have any tattoos but, I would like the following types of tattoos:

_____

_____

_____

_____

_____

16. I have the following number of piercings _____ and they are located:

_____

_____

I do not have any piercings but I would like to pierce this part of my body _____

_____

Because: _____

_____

_____

17. My greatest joy in life is/was:

_____

_____

18. My greatest memory was:

_____

Because: _____

19. I am most happy when I…

_____

_____

_____

20. Trying to think back as far as I can remember, my very first memory was:

_____

_____

21. My favorite movie when I was younger was:

_____

Because: _____

22 Today, my favorite movie is:

_____

Because: _____

23. Growing up, I had/have a favorite toy or blanket that I could not go anywhere without.

Object: _____

Because: _____

_____

24. There is one toy from my past that I wish I had today:

_____

Because: _____

_____

25. My favorite cartoon as a (c)hild, (t)eenager, and (a)dult is/was:

_____(c)   _____ (t)   _____ (a)

26. I attended _____ Middle School _____ High School

I have fond memories of school because _____

_____

I have terrifying memories of school because _____

_____

27. My favorite subject in high school was/is:

_____

28. My least favorite subject in high school is/was:

_____

Because: _____

29. My best friend growing up was/is:

_____

30. The last time I talked with this person was about:

_____ Days _____ Months _____ Years

Because: _____

31. Today, my best friend forever (BFF) is:

_____

The last time I talked with this person was:

_____

32. My religion is:

_____

My religious preference is:

_____ Because: _____

33. I attend religious services (√) on _____ holidays; _____ Sundays;

_____ do not attend; _____ I wish I went more often; _____ N/A

34. To me, God means this to me:

_____

_____

_____

35. To me, Jesus Christ means this to me:

_____

_____

_____

36. I have this many pets (0-?): _____ fish; _____ cat; _____ dog; _____ (other)

37: If I could have any animal in the world as a pet, it would be a:

_____ Because: _____

38. I want/wanted to be this when I grow up:

_____

Because: _____

39a. I consider myself to be an outgoing person: (√): _____ Yes _____ No
   (If you were); I used to be an outgoing person until:

_____

Because: _____

39b. I prefer to isolate myself from others: (√): _____ Yes _____ No
    (If yes); I prefer to be alone from my friends and family because:

_____

_____

40. My favorite genres of movies are:

_____   _____   _____

41. I do not like to watch these types of movies:

_____   _____   _____

_____   _____   _____

42. I like the following types of music:

_____   _____   _____

_____   _____   _____

43. I do not the following types of music:

_____   _____   _____

_____   _____   _____

44. My favorite actors/actresses are:

_____   _____   _____

_____   _____   _____

45. I really do not like these actors/actresses:

_____   _____   _____

46. I am a (√) _____ **Republican** _____ **Democrat** _____ **Don't Care**

(if outside the USA): _____ **Other**

47. If I could have any type of car in the world, it would be a:

_____

Color: _____

The details would include: _____

_____

_____

48. My first crush was/is: _____

Did/do they know of this crush: _____ Yes _____ No

49. I prefer the (one or more): _____ **Summer** _____ **Fall**

_____ **Spring** _____ **Winter**

Because: _____

_____

50. I like to swim in a: _____ Pool _____ Ocean _____ Lake

_____ River _____ Pond _____ None of the above

51. My favorite holiday is: _____

Because: _____

53. My least favorite holidays are: _____ _____

Because: _____

53. My all-time favorite type of food to eat is: _____

Because: _____

54. My biggest fear in the world is: _____

Because:

_____

55. Two things that I like to do to relax are:

_____

_____

56. My favorite thing to do is: _____

I used to love to do this: _____

But, I no longer do this because: _____

57. If I could have 3 wishes, they would be:

(1) _____

(2) _____

(3) _____

58. I am related to this famous ancestor:

_____

They are known for: _____

59. My lucky number is:

_____

60. If I could visit any place in the world, it would be:

_____

Because: _____

61. I like watching the following sports:

_____   _____   _____

62. I like to play the following sports:

_____   _____   _____

63. I like to watch the following TV shows:

_____   _____   _____

_____   _____   _____

_____   _____   _____

_____   _____   _____

64. My favorite scent is:

_____

Because: _____

65. I have the following hobbies:

_____   _____   _____

_____   _____   _____

66. My proudest moment was when I:

_____

Looking back at that moment, I now feel: _____

_____

67. The last compliment I received was: _____

Because: _____

At the time, I felt: _____

Looking back at it now, I feel: _____

68. My best physical feature is:

_____

Because: _____

69. I have been skydiving: _____ **Yes** _____ **No**

   If no; I would love to go skydiving: _____ Yes _____ No

   If no; I am too scared to go skydiving: _____ Yes _____ No

   The thought of going skydiving, makes me want to: _____

   Now that I think about skydiving, I feel: _____

70. One of my most peaceful memories was when:

_____

_____

_____

71. If I had a superpower, it would be:

_____

Because: _____

72. If I could visit any place in the world, it would be:

_____

Because: _____

73. If I could travel back in time, I would go to:

_____ (year)

Because: _____

_____

74. If I could meet any celebrity (living or dead), they would be:

_____

Because: _____

75. If I were on a deserted island and I could have 4 things and up to 2 people and 1 pet, they would be:

_____ (things)   _____ (things)

_____ (things)   _____ (things)

_____ (person)   _____ (person)

_____ (pet)

76. When I was younger, I was afraid of:

_____

Because: _____

77. These days, I am afraid of:

_____   _____   _____

_____   _____   _____

78. I would rather live … (√)

Alone   ____
W/Family   ____
W/Friends   ____

79. Looking back, I regret: (√)

Things I have done   ____
Things I have not done   ____

80. Looking forward … (√)

I am hopeless of my future   ____
I am hopeful of my future   ____

81. I am hopeful for my future because …

_____

_____

82. The best thing that someone could tell me right now is …

_____

_____

83. The place that I feel most comfortable at is …

_____

Because: _____

84. A place that I do not feel safe at is ….

_____

Because: _____

85. My two pet peeves in life are …

(1) _____

(2) _____

86. If I had to choose 4 words to describe myself, they would be ...

_____   _____

_____   _____

87. My favorite 2 emotions to express are ...

_____   _____

88. My guilty pleasures are:

_____   _____   _____

_____   _____   _____

89. My most embarrassing moment was when ...

_____

_____

90. I am afraid of flying in an airplane: _____ Yes _____ No

91. My goals in life are ...

(1) _____

(2) _____

(3) _____

92. My greatest accomplishments have been:

_____   _____

_____   _____

93. When walking by strangers, I ... (√)

Prefer to look away   _____
I feel comfortable greeting them with a smile   _____
I feel comfortable greeting them with words   _____

94. I have been in therapy in my past: (√) _____ Yes _____ No _____ I need to go back

95. I feel (comfortable / uncomfortable) wearing a swimsuit in public.

96. I feel (supported / unsupported) by my friends and family with my recovery.

97. When taking a shower I prefer ... (√)

The lights on   _____
The lights off   _____
The door closed   _____
The door opened   _____

98. When taking a bath, I prefer ... (√)

Bubbles   _____
No bubbles   _____

99. I sleep better with … (√)

My lights on   _____
My lights off   _____
My bedroom door opened   _____
My bedroom door closed   _____
My closet doors opened   _____
My closet doors closed   _____

100. I currently feel …

_____

_____

NOTES

RECOVERY EXERCISES II:
EMOTIONS & SELF-AWARENESS

Section I: Emotions

1. I tend to keep my emotions bottled up inside: _____ Yes _____ No

2. When I am sad, I like to ....

_____

3. When I am mad, I like to ....

_____

4. When I am upset, I like to ....

_____

5. When I am angry, I like to ...

_____

6. The last funeral I attended was for ...

_____

At the time, I remember feeling ...

_____

7. My opinions about abortion are ...

_____

_____

8. My opinions about the death penalty are ...

_____

_____

9. I describe fears as:

_____

_____

10. I describe anxiety as:

_____

_____

11. I describe phobias as:

_____

_____

12. I describe Post-Traumatic Stress Disorder (PTSD) as:

_____

_____

13. I typically avoid certain places, people, or things that are known triggers for me?

_____ Yes   _____ No

14. I engage in the following to help with my anxiety, fears, phobias, and panic attacks:

_____ Non-prescription Drugs   _____ Illegal Drugs
_____ Alcohol _____ Smoking

15. My anxiety, fears, phobias, and/or PTSD interfere with the following:

_____ Work _____ School _____ Friendships
_____ Family Relationships _____ Romantic Relationships

16. When I look in a mirror, I typically see ...

_____

_____

17. When I look in a mirror, I typically feel ...

_____

_____

18. If I could be any animal in the world, it would be: _____

Because: _____

_____

19. I tend to worry more than I probably should? _____ Yes _____ No

20. For the following exercise, attempt to respond quickly with the first word or phrase that comes to mind:

WATER	FEAR
DRY	ANXIOUS
SAND	DEATH
ICE	CAR WRECK
COLD	WALLS
DAMP	PANIC
DARK	ATTACK
MIRROR	OCEANS
FLOWER	RAGE
RELIGION	BLACK
FAITH	TRUST
GOD	PAIN
YELLOW	EMOTIONS
ORANGE	RAIN
RED	THUNDER
BLUE	PUNCH
LONELINESS	KICK
RELATIONSHIPS	SCREAM
GUNS	LOVE
PUPPY	SCARS
CAT	HIDDEN
BIRD	SHADOWS
FLYING	TERROR
DYING	NIGHTMARE
ME	BULLY
MOTHER	SADNESS
FATHER	GUILT

SLEEP	
BEDROOM	
LOCKED DOOR	
TIME	
VIOLENCE	
HEART POUNDING	
EATING	
FALLING	

LOSS	
STRESS	
TEARS	
PRESSURE	
AVOIDANCE	
PET	
SAFETY OBJECT	
ABUSE	

21. **I am a risk taker:** _____ Yes _____ No
   I used to be a risk taker: _____ Yes _____ No

If no longer a risk taker, it is because:

_____

_____

_____

22. **My positive coping skills include the following:**

_____

_____

_____

23. **If I had to describe myself to a blind person, I would tell them that I …**

_____

_____

_____

24. I have been bullied: _____ Yes _____ No
     I have bullied others: _____ Yes _____ No

25. I like to do the following things to relax:

_____

_____

_____

_____

26. I tend to feel guilty about: _____

_____

27. The thing that scares me the most in life is: _____

_____

28. I have had thought about suicide in the past? (√)

_____ (y) _____ (n)

29. I have had thought about hurting others in the past? (√)

_____ (y) _____ (n)

30. I have had thought about hurting animals in the past? (√)

_____ (y)   _____ (n)

31. In the past I have hurt: (√) _____ people _____ animals _____ self

32. A lie or set of lies that I typically tell myself is/are …

_____

_____

33. When late for an appointment, date, or outing with friends, I will typically (√):

Tell the truth _____   Tell a lie _____

34. I have experimented with the following drugs in the past (without a prescription):

Narcotics (√)
Heroin   ____
Methadone   ____
Opioids   ____
Oxycodone   ____

Stimulants (√)
Amphetamines   ____
Cocaine   ____
Methamphetamine   ____

Depressants (√)
Barbiturates   ____
Benzodiazepines
(Xanax, Klonipin,
Volume, Ativan)   ____

Hallucinogens (√)
Ecstasy   ____
Ketamine (Special K)   ____
LSD   ____
Marijuana   ____
Steroids   ____
Inhalants   ____

35. I tend to drink alcoholic beverages the following number of times per month (√):

0—1   ____   Unsure   ____
2—5   ____   I am a social drinker   ____
6—8   ____   I use alcohol to self-medicate   ____
9—12   ____   I have been sober for ___ Months
12+   ____   I have been sober for ___ Years

36a.   **I have been cheated on by a significant other in my past** ____ Yes ____ No
36b.   **I have cheated on a significant other in the past**   ____ Yes ____ No

If so, afterwards I felt…

(a) _____

(b)_____

37. The thing that worries me the most in my life is: _____

_____

38. I consider myself this: (√)

_____ Heterosexual _____ Homosexual
_____ Bisexual   _____ Transgender _____ Unsure

39. I am homophobic: _____ Yes _____ No

40. If I were to date someone outside of my race, my family would most likely …

_____

41. I describe racism as ....

_____

_____

_____

42. I am prejudice against ...

_____

_____

_____

43. If I was writing a book about my life, the title would be called?

_____

44. The worst crime against humanity is ....

_____

45. I have been sexually touched (fondled, assaulted) inappropriately by a family member in the past:

_____ Yes   _____ No

If yes, the name of this personal is/was: _____

They are this relation to me: _____

46a. I was sexually assaulted by a family member and at the time; it made me feel …

_____

_____

_____

46b. Looking back at my child molestation victimization, today I feel …

_____

_____

_____

_____

47. I define rape as ….

_____

_____

_____

48. Three things I do not like about myself are …

_____   _____   _____

Because: _____

Because: _____

Because: _____

49. My known triggers are:

_____

_____

_____

_____

_____

50. To me, God is: _____

_____

_____

51. I have a loving bond with my (√)

Mother: _____ (y) _____ (n) _____ (n/a)
Father: _____ (y) _____ (n) _____ (n/a)
Brother: _____ (y) _____ (n) _____ (n/a)
Sister: _____ (y) _____ (n) _____ (n/a)

Maternal Grandfather: _____ (y) _____ (n) _____ (n/a)
Maternal Grandmother: _____ (y) _____ (n) _____ (n/a)
Paternal Grandfather: _____ (y) _____ (n) _____ (n/a)
Paternal Grandmother: _____ (y) _____ (n) _____ (n/a)

52. My mother has said that she loves me an adequate amount of over the years?

_____ (y) _____ (n)

53. My father has said that he loves me an adequate amount of over the years?

_____ (y) _____ (n)

54. There is at least one family member who has done something to me that I still cannot forgive them for:

Name: _____ Relationship: _____

Act: _____

55. My favorite relative is:

Name: _____ Relationship: _____

Because: _____

56. There is one relative who I cannot stand:

Name: _____ Relationship: _____

Because: _____

57. I have a friend who has betrayed me: _____ Yes _____ No

Because: _____

I have forgiven them: _____ (Yes) _____ (No)

58. I have been harassed or bullied by the following people …

(1) _____

(2) _____

59. My 3 worst qualities are …

(1) _____

 Because: _____

(2) _____

Because: _____

(3) _____

Because: _____

60. I define recovery as …

_____

_____

_____

61. An animal that best describes me is …

_____

Because: _____

62. I have learned the following lesson the hard way:

_____

63. The following really gets under my skin:

_____

Reason: _____

64. I hate it when other people ….

_____

65. I get so mad when …

_____

66. I feel like other people just do not understand me: _____ Yes _____ No

(If yes); because: _____

67. I have cut (cutting) in the past (√): _____ Yes _____ No _____ I have thought about it

If so, because …

_____

_____

68. People have teased me about my weight: _____ Yes _____ No

69. I prefer (√): _____ Darkness _____ Daylight _____ Both

70. I have _____ (#) tattoos _____ (#) piercings

71. I tend to feel hopeful more than I should feel hopeful: _____ Yes _____ No

72. I get panic attacks: _____ Yes _____ No

If yes; when I have panic attacks, I typically experience the following:

PHYSICAL EXPERIENCES	MENTAL EXPERIENCES

73. My triggers are [for each]:

ANXIETY	FEARS	PHOBIAS	PTSD

74. I am haunted by the memory of ....

_____

Because: _____

_____

75. One of my most tragic memories was when …

_____

Because: _____

_____

76. A memory that has angered me for years is …

_____

Because: _____

_____

77. One of my fondest childhood memories was …

_____

Because: _____

78. My biggest fear is …

_____

Because: _____

79. Something that has been on my mind lately has been …

_____

Because: _____

80. When I think of the date 9-11-01, I feel …

_____

_____

_____

81. I have served in the military: _____ Yes _____ No _____ Plan to

82. I am a disabled veteran: _____ Yes _____ No

If so; _____ Physical _____ Psychological

83. I have Post-Traumatic Stress Disorder (PTSD) related to combat: _____ Yes ____ No

84. I suffer from military related survivor's guilt: _____ Yes ____ No

85. I suffer from other than military related survivor's guilt: _____ Yes ____ No

86. If you answered NO to questions 83 – 85, skip this section. If you answered YES to any of these questions; it is because I feel:

_____

_____

_____

_____

Survivor's Guilt is a normal psychological condition when someone believes that they should have been the person to die instead of those who did. This is a common occurrence with survivors of combat, fatal car accidents, friends/family members of suicides, natural disasters, and even terrorist-related events such as the attacks of 9/11 or survivors of school massacres. You are not alone and there are therapists, counselors, psychologists, and psychiatrists who specialize in this type of trauma therapy. You do not need to do this by yourself. Prolonged survivor's guilt can lead to addictions such as illegal drugs and prescription abuse, anorexia and bulimia, alcohol abuse, self-harming behaviors such as cutting and risk taking. Other symptoms may include but are not limited to anger, denial, fear, phobias, panic attacks, suicidal and homicidal idealizations.

87. I feel like I am losing my grip with reality: _____ Yes _____ No

88. I am worried what my family and friends will think of me if I ask for professional help to treat my anxiety, fears, phobias, or PTSD: _____ Yes _____ No

If you answered yes, then please do not let this hesitation prevent you from seeking the help that you need. It should not matter to you what other people think of you. I realize this is easier said than done when it comes to family and friends because you probably want them to befriend you and perceive you as mentally stable; but when it comes to mental blocks, addictions, mood swings, anxiety, fears, phobias, and panic attacks – especially PTSD related panic attacks, we tend to distort reality and in turn we put up defensive walls around us, shutting out the very people we need in our life. Unfortunately, you cannot always take to heart what other people think or feel about you, especially if your mental blocks have distorted this perception of them.

If your friends and family are aware of past anxieties, fears, phobias, etc., and they have teased you about how or why 'they think' you suffer from it; then this is often their reality and not yours. For example, if you suffer from combat related PTSD, then those closest to you may never truly understand what it is that you have been through; and even if they have served in the military, this does not mean that every soldier will have the same experiences.

I suffered from bulimia for about 9-years and I cannot count the number of times that someone has said to me; *"Oh, just stop sticking your finger down your throat, it's that easy!"* Believe me, I can say first hand that it is not that easy. If it were that easy, there would be less people suffering from eating disorders; of course, it is easy for someone who has never experienced bulimia to make these types of snap judgments. The point is, you cannot always control what other people think or feel, accept or validate about you because that is their reality not yours.

Section II: Interpersonal Self-Assessment

Use a (√) to reflect your response.

1. I do not like to talk about myself: _____ (y) _____ (n) _____ (unsure)
2. I have difficulty asking for help: _____ (y) _____ (n) _____ (unsure)
3. I would rather be by myself than with others: _____ (y) _____ (n) _____ (unsure)
4. I have difficulty interacting with others: _____ (y) _____ (n) _____ (unsure)
5. I often say NO when I want to say YES: _____ (y) _____ (n) _____ (unsure)
6. I often say YES when I want to say NO: _____ (y) _____ (n) _____ (unsure)
7. I tend to feel overwhelmed when helping others: _____ (y) _____ (n) _____ (unsure)
8. I tend to feel overwhelmed easily: _____ (y) _____ (n) _____ (unsure)
9. If I feel overwhelmed, I do not say anything: _____ (y) _____ (n) _____ (unsure)
10. I get bothered easily but do not say anything: _____ (y) _____ (n) _____ (unsure)
11. I get bothered easily but I am scared to say something: _____ (y) _____ (n) _____ (unsure)
12. I get irritable easily: _____ (y) _____ (n) _____ (unsure)
13. I prefer to keep my emotions bottled up: _____ (y) _____ (n) _____ (unsure)
14. I yell and snap at people a lot: _____ (y) _____ (n) _____ (unsure)
15. People just do not understand me: _____ (y) _____ (n) _____ (unsure)
16. If people tell me NO, I get angry: _____ (y) _____ (n) _____ (unsure)
17. I often say YES to those who usually says NO to me: _____ (y) _____ (n) _____ (unsure)
18. I have crying spells for no known reason: _____ (y) _____ (n) _____ (unsure)
19. I feel sad or depressed a lot: _____ (y) _____ (n) _____ (unsure)
20. I feel happy a lot: _____ (y) _____ (n) _____ (unsure)
21. I have difficulty making eye contact when talking: _____ (y) _____ (n) _____ (unsure)
22. I have difficulty expressing my feelings to others: _____ (y) _____ (n) _____ (unsure)
23. I try to be the center of attention around others: _____ (y) _____ (n) _____ (unsure)
24. I have difficulty making new friends: _____ (y) _____ (n) _____ (unsure)
25. I have compulsive behaviors: _____ (y) _____ (n) _____ (unsure)
26. I tend to worry about my physical health: _____ (y) _____ (n) _____ (unsure)
27. I tend to worry about my mental health: _____ (y) _____ (n) _____ (unsure)
28. I tend to worry about my family: _____ (y) _____ (n) _____ (unsure)
29. I tend to worry about my friends: _____ (y) _____ (n) _____ (unsure)
30. I tend to worry about intimate relationships: _____ (y) _____ (n) _____ (unsure)
31. I tend to worry about my past a lot: _____ (y) _____ (n) _____ (unsure)
32. I tend to worry about my future a lot: _____ (y) _____ (n) _____ (unsure)
33. I tend to worry about my finances: _____ (y) _____ (n) _____ (unsure)

34. I tend to worry about my education/grades: _____ (y) _____ (n) _____ (unsure)
35. I tend to worry about other health issues: _____ (y) _____ (n) _____ (unsure)
36. I tend to worry about my legal issues: _____ (y) _____ (n) _____ (unsure)
37. I tend to worry about finding a job: _____ (y) _____ (n) _____ (unsure)
38. I tend to worry about getting fired: _____ (y) _____ (n) _____ (unsure)
39. I tend to worry about my weight: _____ (y) _____ (n) _____ (unsure)
40. I tend to worry about my place in society: _____ (y) _____ (n) _____ (unsure)
41. I tend to over exaggerate things: _____ (y) _____ (n) _____ (unsure)
42. I have anxiety: _____ (y) _____ (n) _____ (unsure)
43. I have fears: _____ (y) _____ (n) _____ (unsure)
44. I have phobias: _____ (y) _____ (n) _____ (unsure)
45. I have been diagnosed with PTSD: _____ (y) _____ (n) _____ (unsure)
46. I experience 2 or more Panic Attacks a month: _____ (y) _____ (n) _____ (unsure)
47. I have short term memory problems: _____ (y) _____ (n) _____ (unsure)
48. I have long term memory problems: _____ (y) _____ (n) _____ (unsure)
49. I have difficulties concentrating: _____ (y) _____ (n) _____ (unsure)
50. I do not like to talk about myself to others: _____ (y) _____ (n) _____ (unsure)

Section III: SELF-AWARENESS

For the following questions respond with a √ (1) for yes/true and (2) for no/false.

1. Tattoos are a form of cutting _____ (1) _____ (2)
2. I have thought about cutting in my past _____ (1) _____ (2)
3. I cut when I feel anxious _____ (1) _____ (2)
4. I cut when I feel scared _____ (1) _____ (2)
5. I have had thoughts about suicide in my past _____ (1) _____ (2)
6. I often feel ashamed _____ (1) _____ (2)
7. I have thought about hurting others _____ (1) _____ (2)
8. I have been sexually assaulted _____ (1) _____ (2)
9. I have had night terrors in my past _____ (1) _____ (2)
10. I have had nightmares in my past _____ (1) _____ (2)
11. I have had crying spells in my past _____ (1) _____ (2)
12. I have uncontrollable crying spells _____ (1) _____ (2)
13. I often worry about what others think of me _____ (1) _____ (2)
14. I get distracted easily _____ (1) _____ (2)
15. I tend to feel like someone is watching me _____ (1) _____ (2)
16. I tend to worry a lot _____ (1) _____ (2)
17. I am a failure _____ (1) _____ (2)
18. I tend to be sad a lot _____ (1) _____ (2)
19. I love myself _____ (1) _____ (2)
20. I feel loved by others _____ (1) _____ (2)
21. I have low self-esteem issues _____ (1) _____ (2)
22. I have more male friends than female _____ (1) _____ (2)
23. I have more female friends than male _____ (1) _____ (2)
24. I hate to be seen in a swimsuit _____ (1) _____ (2)
25. I like to daydream _____ (1) _____ (2)
26. I have an extreme fear of gaining weight _____ (1) _____ (2)
27. I prefer to keep my emotions bottled up _____ (1) _____ (2)
28. I prefer isolation _____ (1) _____ (2)
29. I prefer to be around others _____ (1) _____ (2)
30. I tend to feel dizzy a lot _____ (1) _____ (2)
31. I tend to experience fatigue a lot _____ (1) _____ (2)
32. I feel like there is a dark cloud over me _____ (1) _____ (2)
33. I prefer to be alone rather than sociable _____ (1) _____ (2)

34. I tend to experience chest pains when anxious _____ (1) _____ (2)

35. I tend to experience chest pains when scared _____ (1) _____ (2)

36. I tend to be quite irritable around others _____ (1) _____ (2)

37. I like helping others _____ (1) _____ (2)

38. I like others who help me _____ (1) _____ (2)

39. I like to fly in an airplane _____ (1) _____ (2)

40. I like to go swimming in an ocean _____ (1) _____ (2)

41. I tend to have low blood pressure _____ (1) _____ (2)

42. I tend to feel cold even during hot weather _____ (1) _____ (2)

43. I feel like I have no control over my life _____ (1) _____ (2)

44. I have a fear of falling _____ (1) _____ (2)

45. I have a fear of dying _____ (1) _____ (2)

46. I have a fear of crowds' _____ (1) _____ (2)

47. I have a fear of eating in public _____ (1) _____ (2)

48. I have a fear of gaining weight _____ (1) _____ (2)

49. If I gain weight, my self-esteem goes down _____ (1) _____ (2)

50. I do not deserve happiness _____ (1) _____ (2)

51. I have survivor's guilt _____ (1) _____ (2)

52. I have served in the military _____ (1) _____ (2)

53. I have lost a spouse/partner _____ (1) _____ (2)

54. I have lost a close friend _____ (1) _____ (2)

55. I have lost a boy/girlfriend _____ (1) _____ (2)

56. I try to suppress my emotions to avoid them _____ (1) _____ (2)

57. I am often anxious, stressed, or depressed _____ (1) _____ (2)

58. I get bored easily _____ (1) _____ (2)

59. I tend to be a procrastinator _____ (1) _____ (2)

60. I should act on my feelings rather than hide it _____ (1) _____ (2)

61. I do not like to have pictures taken of me _____ (1) _____ (2)

62. If I pose for a picture, I prefer it be a head shot _____ (1) _____ (2)

63. I worry about other people more than I _____ (1) _____ (2)

64. I worry about my life more than lives of others _____ (1) _____ (2)

65. I believe in God/Christ _____ (1) _____ (2)

66. I am an Atheist _____ (1) _____ (2)

67. I worry about my finances _____ (1) _____ (2)

68. I worry about my grades in school _____ (1) _____ (2)

69. I hate it when someone says I gained weight _____ (1) _____ (2)

70. I hate it when someone says I lost weight _____ (1) _____ (2)

71. I have been emotionally abused _____ (1) _____ (2)

72. I have been sexually abused   _____ (1)   _____ (2)

73. I have been verbally abused   _____ (1)   _____ (2)

74. I have been assaulted   _____ (1)   _____ (2)

75. I have been sexually assaulted   _____ (1)   _____ (2)

76. I have been raped   _____ (1)   _____ (2)

77. I have been sexually harassed   _____ (1)   _____ (2)

78. I have been racially harassed   _____ (1)   _____ (2)

79. I have issues with body image   _____ (1)   _____ (2)

80. I struggle with personal imperfection   _____ (1)   _____ (2)

81. I feel unsafe by myself   _____ (1)   _____ (2)

82. I feel unsafe where I live   _____ (1)   _____ (2)

83. I hate life   _____ (1)   _____ (2)

84. I am scared of driving   _____ (1)   _____ (2)

85. I have a fear of germs   _____ (1)   _____ (2)

86. I have a fear of heights   _____ (1)   _____ (2)

87. I have a fear of dogs'   _____ (1)   _____ (2)

88. I have a fear of cats'   _____ (1)   _____ (2)

89. I have been SAVED in Christ   _____ (1)   _____ (2)

90. I have a fear of men   _____ (1)   _____ (2)

91. I have a fear of women   _____ (1)   _____ (2)

92. I like to meditate   _____ (1)   _____ (2)

93. I like to read   _____ (1)   _____ (2)

94. I never feel clean enough   _____ (1)   _____ (2)

95. I am an emotional eater   _____ (1)   _____ (2)

96. I have a fear of getting older   _____ (1)   _____ (2)

97. I am aware of my triggers   _____ (1)   _____ (2)

98. I have safe foods   _____ (1)   _____ (2)

99. I like to journal   _____ (1)   _____ (2)

100. I feel that I have control of my life   _____ (1)   _____ (2)

Section IV

Use this section to write down anything that you feel you have little or no control that often leads to anxiety or panic attacks

(1) _____

(2) _____

(3) _____

(4) _____

If I could replace the above anxieties with a positive coping skill, I would rather:

(1) _____

_____

(2) _____

_____

(3) _____

_____

(4) _____

_____

Section V
(Victims of sexual abuse, sexual assault, and domestic violence)

If you are still having difficulty find words to journal about, then try writing an angry letter to your abuser/offender. Think of a strong emotion that would normally cause you much distress about the incident or person and harness that emotion for several minutes just to the point of anxiety or a panic attack and use that emotion to write an angry letter to that person about how you really feel about them. There is no right or wrong response here and no guilt to feel afterwards. If anything, you should feel empowered and as if a weight has been lifted from your deep within your mind and body. This exercise is all about 'your' empowerment and the ability to take back some control in your life. Imagine that the person of all your anxiety and negative emotions is standing in front of you and take a deep breath or two and remember they are not really there. This is all about you; they cannot hurt you. Rather than feel any fear from them, stand up and tell them how you really feel! Just let your raw emotions pour out even if not in complete sentences – just write it out. Afterwards, I recommend burning the letter and disposing of it safely (age appropriate in the use of fire). When you burn the letter, try to imagine that any leftover anxieties, fears, or related emotions have left your body—up in smoke!

If you need help getting started, try using the: How, What, Where, Why, and the Who. You can repeat this exercise any time you need to reinforce your recovery process.

_____

_____

_____

_____

_____

_____

_____

Section VI

=============================

Reflection Exercise I: Accountability

I recommend using this exercise to gage how you are feeling and what you are thinking about leading up to an anxiety episode or panic attack. . Use the last column to check whether or not it was related to PTSD.

	EMOTIONS	THOUGHTS	PHYSICAL PAIN	(√)
1				
2				
3				
4				
5				
6				
7				
8				

J A N U A R Y

9			
10			
11			
12			
13			
14			
15			
16			
17			
18			
19			
20			
21			
22			
23			

24			
25			
26			
27			
28			
29			
30			
31			

F	1			
E	2			
B	3			
R	4			
U	5			
A	6			
R	7			
Y	8			
	9			
	10			
	11			
	12			
	13			
	14			

15			
16			
17			
18			
19			
20			
21			
22			
23			
24			
25			
26			
27			
28			

29				

1			
2			
3			
4			
5			
6			
7			
8			
9			
10			
11			
12			
13			
14			

15			
16			
17			
18			
19			
20			
21			
22			
23			
24			
25			
26			
27			
28			

29			
30			
31			

A P R I L

1				
2				
3				
4				
5				
6				
7				
8				
9				
10				
11				
12				
13				
14				

15			
16			
17			
18			
19			
20			
21			
22			
23			
24			
25			
26			
27			
28			

29			
30			

MAY				
1				
2				
3				
4				
5				
6				
7				
8				
9				
10				
11				
12				
13				
14				

15			
16			
17			
18			
19			
20			
21			
22			
23			
24			
25			
26			
27			
28			

29			
30			
31			

JUNE

1				
2				
3				
4				
5				
6				
7				
8				
9				
10				
11				
12				
13				
14				

15			
16			
17			
18			
19			
20			
21			
22			
23			
24			
25			
26			
27			
28			

29			
30			

1			
2			
3			
4			
5			
6			
7			
8			
9			
10			
11			
12			
13			
14			

JULY

15			
16			
17			
18			
19			
20			
21			
22			
23			
24			
25			
26			
27			
28			

29			
30			
31			

1				
2				
3				
4				
5				
6				
7				
8				
9				
10				
11				
12				
13				
14				

15			
16			
17			
18			
19			
20			
21			
22			
23			
24			
25			
26			
27			
28			

29				
30				
31				

S E P T E N B E R

1			
2			
3			
4			
5			
6			
7			
8			
9			
10			
11			
12			
13			
14			

15			
16			
17			
18			
19			
20			
21			
22			
23			
24			
25			
26			
27			
28			

29			
30			

OCTOBER

1				
2				
3				
4				
5				
6				
7				
8				
9				
10				
11				
12				
13				
14				

15			
16			
17			
18			
19			
20			
21			
22			
23			
24			
25			
26			
27			
28			

29			
30			
31			

NOVEMBER

1				
2				
3				
4				
5				
6				
7				
8				
9				
10				
11				
12				
13				
14				

15			
16			
17			
18			
19			
20			
21			
22			
23			
24			
25			
26			
27			
28			

29			
30			

	1			
	2			
	3			
	4			
	5			
	6			
	7			
	8			
	9			
	10			
	11			
	12			
	13			
	14			

15			
16			
17			
18			
19			
20			
21			
22			
23			
24			
25			
26			
27			
28			

29			
30			
31			

Reflection Exercise II: Self-Awareness

Now that you have experienced the anxiety episode or panics attack. I recommend using this exercise to gage how you felt after it passed. Use the last column to check whether you used a positive coping skill to help with the episode or attack.

	EMOTIONS	THOUGHTS	PHYSICAL PAIN	(√)
1				
2				
3				
4				
5				
6				
7				
8				
9				
10				

J
A
N
U
A
R
Y

11				
12				
13				
14				
15				
16				
17				
18				
19				
20				
21				
22				
23				
24				
25				

26			
27			
28			
29			
30			
31			

1				
2				
3				
4				
5				
6				
7				
8				
9				
10				
11				
12				
13				
14				
15				

FEBRUARY

16			
17			
18			
19			
20			
21			
22			
23			
24			
25			
26			
27			
28			

29				

MARCH

1				
2				
3				
4				
5				
6				
7				
8				
9				
10				
11				
12				
13				
14				
15				

16			
17			
18			
19			
20			
21			
22			
23			
24			
25			
26			
27			
28			

29			
30			
31			

A P R I L

1			
2			
3			
4			
5			
6			
7			
8			
9			
10			
11			
12			
13			
14			

15			
16			
17			
18			
19			
20			
21			
22			
23			
24			
25			
26			
27			
28			

29			
30			

M
A
Y

1				
2				
3				
4				
5				
6				
7				
8				
9				
10				
11				
12				
13				
14				
15				

16			
17			
18			
19			
20			
21			
22			
23			
24			
25			
26			
27			
28			

29			
30			
31			

JUNE

1				
2				
3				
4				
5				
6				
7				
8				
9				
10				
11				
12				
13				
14				

15			
16			
17			
18			
19			
20			
21			
22			
23			
24			
25			
26			
27			
28			

29			
30			

1			
2			
3			
4			
5			
6			
7			
8			
9			
10			
11			
12			
13			
14			

15			
16			
17			
18			
19			
20			
21			
22			
23			
24			
25			
26			
27			

28				
29				
30				
31				

AUGUST

1				
2				
3				
4				
5				
6				
7				
8				
9				
10				
11				
12				
13				

14			
15			
16			
17			
18			
19			
20			
21			
22			
23			
24			
25			
26			
27			

28			
29			
30			
31			

S E P T E M B E R

1				
2				
3				
4				
5				
6				
7				
8				
9				
10				
11				
12				
13				
14				

15			
16			
17			
18			
19			
20			
21			
22			
23			
24			
25			
26			
27			
28			

29			
30			

O C T O B E R

1				
2				
3				
4				
5				
6				
7				
8				
9				
10				
11				
12				
13				
14				

15			
16			
17			
18			
19			
20			
21			
22			
23			
24			
25			
26			
27			
28			

29				
30				
31				

N	1			
O	2			
V	3			
E	4			
M	5			
B	6			
E	7			
R	8			
	9			
	10			
	11			
	12			
	13			
	14			

15			
16			
17			
18			
19			
20			
21			
22			
23			
24			
25			
26			
27			
28			

29			
30			

D E C E M B E R

1				
2				
3				
4				
5				
6				
7				
8				
9				
10				
11				
12				
13				
14				

15			
16			
17			
18			
19			
20			
21			
22			
23			
24			
25			
26			
27			
28			

29			
30			
31			

REFLECTION EXERCISE III: Trigger Awareness

==================================

Use the following exercise to target your emotions and physical pain associated with each.

TRIGGER ASSOCIATION

EMOTION / SYMPTOM / THOUGHT	STRESSORS OFTEN ASSOCIATED WITH EMOTION	PHYSICAL SYMPTOMS OFTEN ASSOCIATED WITH EMOTION	CAUSES FLASHBACKS (√)	CAUSES SUICIDAL THOUGHTS (√)
ANGER				
ANXIOUS				
CLAMMY HANDS				
COLDNESS				
DEPRESSION				
FATIGUE				
FRIGHTENED				
HAPPINESS				
HOT FLASHES				

IRRITABLE / HOSTILE				
MANIA				
MUSCLE ACHES				
POUNDING HEAT RATE				
SADNESS				
SHOULDER TIGHTNESS				
STRESS				
TENSION				

REFLECTION EXERCISE IV: Word Association (Self-Awareness)

===

For this exercise, write down the first word or thought that comes to mind for each of the following words.

WORD	RESPONSE
FORGOTTEN	
DRAINED	
EXPOSED	
ABANDONED	
ANXIOUS	
AFRAID	
JEALOUS	

GRIEF	
AGGRESSIVE	
AGONY	
ABUSED	
ASSAULTED	
DISGUSTED	
APATHY	
SYMPATHY	
ASHAMED	
TOUCHED	
HELPLESS	

VULNERABLE	
AGGRAVATED	
IRRITATED	
HORRIFIED	
NERVOUS	
ALARMED	
OBSESSIONS	
COMPULSIONS	

REFLECTIONE EXERCISE V: Charting My Emotions

===

For this exercise, try to make a list of what you feel represents your typical positive and negative emotions.

My Positive Emotions	My Negative Emotions

The following things drive me freaking crazy:

_____

_____

_____

_____

_____

The following things that other people do that drives me freaking crazy are:

_____

_____

REFLECTION EXERCISE VI: Fears, Phobias, Anxiety, Panic Attacks, PTSD

My Fears	I Typically try to avoid It (√)	Positive Reinforcements or Distractions I can try to do to help reduce my Fears

My Phobias	I Typically try to avoid It (√)	Positive Reinforcements or Distractions I can try to do to help reduce my Phobias

My Anxieties	I Typically try to avoid known triggers (√)	Positive Reinforcements or Distractions I can try to do to help reduce my Anxiety

My Panic Attacks	I Typically try to avoid known triggers (√)	Positive Reinforcements or Distractions I can try to do to help reduce my Panic Attacks

My PTSD Triggers	I Typically try to avoid known triggers (√)	Positive Reinforcements or Distractions I can try to do to help reduce my PTSD Episodes

When I experience PTSD episodes, I typically feel the following:

EMOTIONS / THOUGHTS	PHYSICAL SYMPTOMS

I typically feel like I am living in the Past: _____ Yes _____ No

I have difficulty living in the Present: _____ Yes _____ No

I am very Hopeful / Hopeless about my Future: _____ Yes _____ No

NOTES

NOTES

NOTES

NOTES

Made in the USA
Middletown, DE
04 February 2015